Don't Just Dream About Success: Stack the Odds in Your Favor

Joe Ben Hoyle, President of CPAreviewforFREE

Associate Professor of Accounting, Robins School of Business, University of Richmond

"If your dreams do not scare you, they are not big enough."

Ellen Johnson Sirleaf, President of Liberia
2011 Commencement Address,
Harvard University

This book is dedicated to
my grandchildren:
Emma, Noah,
Lily, and Charlotte

The future of our world depends on the dreams of
today's young people and their ability
to turn those dreams
into success.

About the Author

Joe Ben Hoyle is cofounder and president of CPA Review for FREE. The company has provided free preparatory material for the Certified Public Accounting (CPA) exam since 2008 to offset the high cost of entering the public accounting profession. He is also an associate professor of accounting at the Robins School of Business at the University of Richmond. He is in his 43rd year as a college professor and has won many awards and recognitions over those years.

-- Named one of nine favorite professors in the United States by *Bloomberg BusinessWeek*, September 10, 2012.

--Named the Virginia Professor of the Year in 2007 by the Council for the Advancement and Support of Education.

--Coauthor of *Advanced Accounting* published by McGraw-Hill and now in its 12th edition.

--Coauthor of *Financial Accounting* published by FlatworldKnowledge and now in its 2nd edition.

--Named one of the 100 most influential people in the accounting profession by *Accounting Today* (2009)

--Blog "Getting the Most from Your Students," named the Accounting Education Innovation of the Year for 2013 by the American Accounting Association.

--Named one of 22 favorite professors in the United States by *Business Week*, September 19, 2006.

--Named Distinguished Educator at the University of Richmond five times: 1982, 1986, 1989, 1992, and 1998

Foreword

Bold Dreams, Bold Success

Success always starts with a dream. The bolder the dream, the bolder the success can be.

We all have dreams of success. They fuel our enthusiasm and fire up our imagination. As a long-time teacher, I have listened to college students describe countless dreams ranging from the touching to the grandiose. However, the dream of one particular student simply blew all the rest away.

One beautiful spring day, about a decade ago, that student knocked on my office door. It was near the end of his junior year. I assumed we were going to chat about course selections for the upcoming semester. Instead, he walked in and quietly explained that he was dropping out of school. That began a fantastical story—like a thrilling adventure from a Harry Potter book.

Students sometimes leave college in their freshmen year because they miss family or have a romantic attachment back home. Others face serious monetary issues or discover that college is more work or less fun than they expected. Withdrawal early in a college career is sad news but not necessarily devastating. Steve Jobs dropped out of Reed College after six months. Bill Gates lasted a bit longer before leaving Harvard. Both managed to get by fairly well without a diploma. But, few students leave school at the end of the junior year, especially if they are in good academic standing.

Pulling up a chair, he asked how much I knew about mountain climbing and whether I had heard of the 7 Sisters. I confessed total ignorance except that the sport appeared to be extremely cold, difficult, and dangerous. The term "7 Sisters" drew a complete blank.

The previous summer, he joined a mountain climbing expedition and found the experience so exhilarating that he could hardly wait to climb again. Since then, he had searched for a personal goal to challenge this newfound passion. He explained that "7 Sisters" is a title applied to seven mountains, the highest peaks on each of the seven continents—Everest in Asia, Kilimanjaro in Africa, McKinley in North America, etc. His goal was to become the youngest person to reach the top of all seven.

What a dream! Scale the tallest mountain on each of the seven continents AND do so quickly enough to claim the title of youngest climber to ever accomplish the feat. The sheer audacity was impressive. For many of his fellow students, the biggest challenge in life at that moment was picking a destination for beach week.

Questions came rolling out: Is this idea as dangerous as it sounds? What is the cost? Will you be alone or have companions? How quickly must you start in order to break the record?

Who could not be intrigued? People rarely have the nerve to tackle a goal of this magnitude. *Too often, we settle for dreams that merely scratch the surface of our abilities and then wonder why we are dissatisfied with the results.*

To raise the money necessary for travel and equipment, he needed to leave school as soon as the semester was finished and had stopped in to say good-bye. I wished him well as he walked away and wondered if I would ever see him again. As a fun activity, this was certainly not stamp collecting.

Within a few weeks, I began following his race around the world on an Internet website: North America, Asia, Europe, Africa, and Australia. He relayed stories from exotic places like Katmandu. They sounded more like scenes from an Indiana Jones movie than the actions of a college student. Even for a young person, the physical toll had to be almost beyond belief. The excursion seemed to go well for several months but he encountered serious problems in South America. Within a few hundred yards of the summit in Argentina, bad weather and breathing difficulties forced him to turn back.

At that point, his only option was to regroup and try the entire ascent again. On the second attempt, he successfully reached the top of the sixth of the 7 Sisters. But, the delay cost him vital time. Now behind schedule, he missed the climbing season in Antarctica and lost the chance to set the record. The adventure was over. He returned to college and finished earning his degree. Win, lose or draw, his life had changed forever.

From my perspective, he was a relatively normal young person who set out to accomplish an extraordinary feat. If I ever create a "Hall of Fame for Bold Dreamers," he will be the first inductee. The goal was truly impressive—worthy of a supreme effort. *We should all latch on to dreams that push us toward greatness.* You (yes, YOU) can do that. During your days on this planet, the mark you make is only limited by your ability to dream.

One key question remains: Was this student any less successful because he did not break the record?

Of course not! Success is never about breaking records. Records come and go, but that life-changing effort will be a point of pride forever. Great dreams inspire great efforts. Great efforts lead to great achievements. Finishing first is not necessary in a genuine success story.

What is your dream? Is it truly bold? Have you developed a mindset that will help you succeed regardless of the degree of difficulty? As Washington Irving wrote over 150 years ago, "Great minds have purposes; others have wishes." That sentiment was true then. It is just as true today.

This student had a dream that stretched him to the limit. That is how life should work. Our reaction to such dreams can make the difference between a life well-lived and one that never quite achieves its potential. Success is not attained by accident. It requires an overall philosophy, a personal approach that inspires serious dreams, and the actions necessary to make them come to life. This book is designed to help you articulate and then live that philosophy.

Unfortunately, for many people, "dreams" and "success" are mere words to be repeated like a prayer with no follow-up action. I want you to become a bold dreamer. But, never allow yourself to be satisfied with mere dreams. Get out of the ruts that trap you. Use the tools and mental discipline described throughout this book to empower yourself and make those dreams come true—not every time, but as often as possible.

"We are such stuff as dreams are made on."
William Shakespeare, *The Tempest*

Joe Hoyle,
President, CPAreviewforFREE

Contents

×

One: Weaving a Tapestry of Success

In 1982, I was on the verge of completing the first edition of my *Advanced Accounting* textbook, a project I now view as a Level-3 success (more about that term in a subsequent story). It was a massive endeavor, requiring three years of almost daily labor. I cranked out thousands of pages on a tiny Royal portable typewriter the color of a robin's egg. At times the work was almost nonstop. One Christmas morning, after opening presents with my wife and children, I spent the next several hours sitting alone at our dining room table, typing on that manuscript. Now that word processing has long ago become universal, the thought of creating so many pages of complex material using such a primitive little machine – meticulously deleting mistakes by hand with a rubber ink eraser – is like a memory from the Stone Age.

As the final pages of the textbook were turned over to the publisher, I sought a fitting quotation to place at the bottom of the title page. A search of several volumes of famous sayings failed to uncover the precise message that I wanted to convey to future readers. One morning, I walked across campus for a haircut. The young barber asked about my day and I described the frustrating failure to locate the perfect introductory thought, the finishing touch for my "epic." She pointed to her Quote of the Day calendar on a nearby table and suggested checking out the current entry. With absolutely no expectation of success, I picked it up, read the following sentence, and almost fell out of the chair.

"The real purpose of books is to trap the mind into doing its own thinking."

Christopher Morley

That *Advanced Accounting* textbook will soon be coming out in its 12th edition and those words still reside on the first page.

This story is provided as a warning. The writings in this volume form a trap, one that is intended to lure you into doing your own thinking because that is the only avenue to real accomplishments. The search for success is a fascinating topic filled with plots and subplots, a psychological mystery that must be unraveled slowly over a lifetime. What a marvelous journey the quest can be. Thinking about each of the individual steps along the way is what really helps stack the odds of success in your favor. That process, when coupled with an adequate level of ambition, offers unlimited possibilities to each of us.

Therefore, the ultimate question underlying the creation of this book is simple: How can I trap your mind into thinking more deeply about success? Over the millennia, this subject has been approached from countless directions. And yet, not enough people today achieve the success they desire. Too many fail when they should succeed. My goal is to offer realistic guidance that can improve your chances of attaining success in the endeavors that truly matter to you.

How should the message be conveyed? I have pondered that challenge long and hard. Writers can arrange their words to form many, varied structural frameworks. Hemingway's novels were constructed differently from those of Faulkner.

I recently read a wonderful volume of short stories, *Everything That Rises Must Converge*, by Flannery O'Connor. The author's style has influenced me here. She describes the people, places, and conflicts of the rural South in, I suppose, the 1940s and 1950s. I grew up in that region during those years and her words connected with me in a personal way. At times, she seemed to be analyzing events as if they were unfolding from the recesses of my own history. She made me think.

My interest in Ms. O'Connor's work of fiction had its origin in a chance encounter: A popular magazine listed this work as the greatest short story collection in history (in the judgment of some group of renowned experts). That was enough for me. Immediately intrigued, I ordered a used copy online and devoured the stories within a few days. Success has always fascinated me. I am drawn inexorably to events and deeds that have proven so successful as to be universally acknowledged as great (or, better still, the greatest). In my opinion, *Casablanca* is the best of all movies (I have marveled at Bogart and Bergman dozens of times) and *Blonde on Blonde* is the epitome of what a modern music album should be. This obsession with success at its highest level is not newly acquired. As a ten year-old, I practically worshipped Mickey Mantle because he was considered by many at the time to be the best baseball player in America (although the actual title probably belonged to Willie Mays).

Ms. O'Connor did not create a novel. No character or event wanders through her writing to form a sIngle story line. She chose not to set up a structure as Margaret Mitchell did in *Gone with the Wind* where Scarlet O'Hara and her love for her father's plantation anchor the entire work. Instead, taken together, O'Connor's nine tales form a brilliant tapestry that enables readers to observe the South of that era from different perspectives and on numerous levels. "Thought provoking" is the term that floated through my mind as I moved from one of her short stories to the next.

I do not pretend to possess the talent or the genius of Flannery O'Connor. But, in laying out my reflections on success, I have sought to follow her lead. *My goal has been to produce a thought provoking tapestry about success.* No attempt has been made to create a book where page always follows page in some rigidly logical progression with one chapter setting up the next. Instead, the following work is composed of essays and stories in what might, at times, appear to be a rather random sequence. By this construction, I am seeking to display a vivid depiction of success with its many facets and mysteries. In life, success is not always tightly structured. Hopefully, elements of the end product will prove to be intriguing because I want you (yes, YOU) to think more deeply about success and become truly engaged by the process. Excitement should be an integral part of this journey. In a word association game, success should always be coupled with exhilaration.

I provide no set definition of success within these pages. No effort (subconscious or otherwise) is made to influence you to seek any particular type of success. Those life-altering judgments belong to you alone. Such real decisions require the thinking that you are being pushed to do.

When they were informed that I was working on a book about success, several colleagues suggested the need for a short catchy tagline at the core that could be repeated ad infinitum in a wide variety of situations. Others urged me to develop a numbered list, for example, the 13 essential steps necessary for growing filthy rich. I have no argument with books that follow either of those models. Given the level of sales over the past several decades, they apparently meet a genuine need. But, those books were not what I felt called to write. Instead, I created a tapestry to describe the attainment of success with the hope that these scenes and descriptions will stimulate your thinking and help you become more successful.

As a long-time college professor, I have a recommendation here at the start. Interaction with this book is necessary for it to have any legitimate influence on your actions. If you read and do no more, then you will never do more. Success comes from being active rather than passive. Throughout the book, I suggest activities. Please do them. I think they will help.

For the most part, each story here is independent. At the end of each one, stop and reflect for a few moments. Take your time. No prize will be awarded for the fastest reading. If success is important, you must give it a sufficient amount of your time. Consider the words and suggestions provided before moving on. Identify three or four thoughts that seem most relevant. What struck you as truly significant? Make your own judgments. Avoid getting locked into an observer role. To change the direction of life, move your responses from the vague to the specific. Do not waste time guessing at my hierarchy. What I believe is not relevant. Order your list, beginning with the idea you felt was most important. Then, write 10 words or less to describe how each selected thought pertains to your life, your future, and your success. Write directly in the margins if you wish so the book is tied permanently with your thoughts. Read with your pen in hand and create a conversation between your thoughts and mine.

Which ideas and suggestions are relevant to you?
How does each of these chosen items connect to your success?

This exercise takes virtually no time but offers several benefits.

- An evaluation is required. Moving through each day, we frequently allow ourselves to serve as passive receivers of information, no better than a voice recorder. Take a step beyond that. Consider each story. What particular elements touched you? Everything else is fluff. Evaluation is a skill worth developing, an essential step in critical thinking. Identifying valid connections is a good starting spot for steering your life toward success.

- Selecting key ideas forces you to consider the possibilities that are available. Otto von Bismarck said that "politics is the art of the possible." I would argue that success is really the art of the possible. Determine what goals can be attained. Decide which to seek and how best to make success happen. Avoid overly complicated perspectives; much of success is no more than setting goals, creating reasonable plans, and taking action. Often, it is not the complexity of the challenge that holds us back, but rather a timid unwillingness to believe in our own abilities to make success happen. .

- The writing of the 10 words ties each chosen concept directly to your life. If you never make that connection, achieving success is a difficult challenge. A critical question to consider: "How can a particular suggestion impact me and my desire to succeed?" That is where true in-depth thinking comes into play.

Thomas Edison kept signs hanging on the walls of his factories with a quotation from the artist Joshua Reynolds: "There is no expedient to which a man will not resort to avoid the real labor of thinking." Moving through this book, you and I need to prove how very wrong those words can be.

Success is out there waiting for you. Figure out the possibilities and begin to stack the odds in your favor using those goals that you want to attain and choose to pursue.

Two: Stop Yearning for Success and Start Achieving It

Pick up a high school yearbook. If it is one where the seniors describe their plans, the level of ambition is likely to be impressive. Graduating students typically want to succeed in college, in careers, in marriage, in sports, and in life in general. Success! Success! Success! That seems to be the mantra of the human race.

In virtually every corner of the world around us, the yearning for success is obvious. Perhaps this longing is an essential component of the evolutionary process, one that keeps the species moving forward. People rarely express an inner need to admire the mediocre or average. No high school senior pines for a life marred by failure. With such intense desire seemingly burned directly into human DNA, the world should be practically overflowing with success stories.

The reality is different. Our world is filled with grave problems. We desperately need many more people who are willing to tackle these challenges and achieve success. That is the driving force behind this book. The planet will only become a better place when a significantly larger percentage of its population becomes successful. Less mediocrity and more success is a critical need. Not everyone can be on the cover of *Time* magazine, but we can all succeed more of the time, starting with you (yes, YOU).

Why listen to me? What do I know? My only response to such reasonable questions is that these writings come from a lifetime of experiences. I taught my first class in college in the fall of 1971. I was 23 years old and probably looked 18. Richard Nixon was president of the United States; the Dow Jones Industrial Average stood at 900. Computers were the size of rooms and gasoline was readily available for 36 cents per gallon.

Over the intervening years, I have had the pleasure of working with approximately 6,000 college students (and another 7,000 or so in live review programs for the Certified Public Accountant [CPA] examination). These students have been funny and sweet and lost and lazy and confused. In other words, they have pretty much represented the population as a whole. A few were absolutely brilliant. Most were normal people trying to unravel the maze we call college (not to mention having to deal with the trepidations created by an adult life steamrolling toward them at breakneck speed). Each struck me as interesting and unique – much like snowflakes.

If those high school yearbooks are to be believed, virtually every one of my many students wished for a serious measure of success. Seeking success, though, is not the same as attaining it. This is hardly an insightful epiphany. College students are very bright and energetic, but such glowing attributes do not ensure success. After all these decades, I am still surprised by how little most of those 6,000 understood the techniques and strategies that could have helped them reach their personal goals. When faced with a difficult new challenge, human efforts often seem ineffective at best and self-defeating at worst. Many cannot even articulate what they mean when discussing the success they claim to desire so fervently. To most, it is merely a vague notion that promises to make them feel good or, at least comfortable, as they move through life. It becomes a chant without meaning.

Student: "I want to achieve success!"
Me: "What does that mean?"
Student: "I don't know, but I really do want to be successful!"

Students are schooled – year after year – in reading, math, geography, science, and a whole host of other subjects. However, society provides sparse guidance on the ways and means of achieving success. Our institutions seem to assume that human beings are born with an innate knowledge of that path. Over the years, I have witnessed little evidence to support that assertion. In simple terms, people crave success, but often appear clueless as to how to make it happen.

This book is about working toward success: success at school, success at work, success at all those challenges and projects that people undertake. It is about attaining success in those areas of life that you

8

view as important. Although that sounds like a marvelous goal, I will begin with a confession: I cannot guarantee that anything in these writings will make you successful. Life simply does not work like that. In fact, you probably should be suspicious of any writer, teacher, speaker, or preacher who claims to hold secret keys to success. Such offers are likely to provide nothing more than snake oil.

Instead of promising success, my goal is to help stack the odds in your favor. Every time you undertake a new endeavor, you have some chance of success. It might be 35 percent or 68 percent but it is rarely zero. *In almost every situation, if all events were to go perfectly, you would succeed.* Never lose sight of that. Unless you are Don Quixote attacking windmills, success is always possible or you would not waste your time.

I am convinced that people can take specific steps to improve their chances for success whenever they encounter the opportunities that life provides. Success is not random. It is not the product of luck. Successful people have learned how to succeed. That can be you. That should be you. With thought and work, you can achieve success a much higher percentage of the time. Start today to nudge the odds upward. Do that and evolve into a winner as you begin to succeed more often: not every time (a truly impossible dream), but more of the time. That is the goal here. That is a goal worth seeking.

Closing Activity: Think of moments in your life when you have been successful. The time can be years ago or just last week. Identify two or three successes that were particularly special. Pause for a moment and mentally relive the excitement. Try to replicate the thrill that you felt deep in your heart. This sense of exhilaration should be ever present in your mind. For successful people, it becomes addictive. What were the key elements that made each success possible? What actions led to the outcome? The basic steps to reach success rarely vary, in any fundamental way, from one endeavor to the next. Assessing your past triumphs helps open the door to future success.

Three: The Three Facets of the Derek Jeter Rule

In so many of the endeavors of life, simply getting started is the first serious obstacle. How do you (yes, YOU) begin the process of stacking the odds of success in your favor whenever each new challenge arises? Perhaps you want to complete a complicated project at work, or earn an A in a difficult course at school, or qualify for a new job, or become an excellent tennis player. What do you really want to accomplish? How can the chance of success be increased from (for example) 35 percent to 68 percent? People just like you do this every day and turn themselves into winners. If they can make it happen, so can you. Other people will begin to point at you and mumble with envy, "That person is a real success story."

This scenario is not a false hope if you learn how to stack the odds in your favor. As is often said, "Success is habit forming." With focused attention, basic common sense, and a positive attitude, the momentum of life can be turned in your direction.

I want to begin this chapter by introducing a personal perspective on success that I have long referred to as "the Derek Jeter Rule." It can keep you grounded to help you avoid the trap of self-defeat.

I tend to be a perfectionist, rarely an ideal attitude for success. No matter what the challenge, success for me is automatically associated with hitting the mark on every attempt. I do not tolerate my own mistakes well. I never start out to make 98; I want to be correct 100 percent of the time. Unfortunately, such a demanding approach to life's challenges can be counterproductive. Too often, I become discouraged, and even quit, when projects do not proceed perfectly because my threshold for success is set so high. If the only options are (a) perfection, (b) failure, or (c) quitting, chances for success will be low. No matter how hard a person works, perfection is a rare event. If I am not careful, this strict interpretation of success holds me back and limits what can be accomplished. The biggest barrier to success is frequently my own perfectionist mindset.

Derek Jeter has been one of the best baseball players in the world since he debuted in the U.S. major leagues in 1995. Over all those years, perhaps no other player has been more acclaimed for greatness. A former manager said of him: "You knew from the start there was something special about him. The way he carried himself, the way he played the game. He's just all about winning." If any person can be called successful in baseball, it is Derek Jeter.

Yet, even in his better years, Jeter rarely hit safely more than 3 times out of every 10 at-bats (a .300 batting average). Season in and season out, seventy percent of his attempts normally end in failure. Despite all those missed opportunities, his accomplishments are still universally praised. Throughout most of baseball's long history, any player who manages three hits on a consistent basis while making seven outs is applauded wildly. The margin, though, is tight. If a teammate makes only two hits during every ten plate appearances rather than three, his batting average is .200 and he probably needs to consider a different career. A base hit 30 percent of the time is exceptional — that person might well be heading to the Hall of Fame — whereas a player with a 20 percent success rate is viewed as a dismal failure.

Over the years, I have repeated the facets of the Derek Jeter Rule to myself thousands of times to keep my drive to succeed properly on track.

(1) — *Perfection is almost never necessary for success.* During his basketball career, Michael Jordan hit less than half his shots. In football, John Elway completed only 56.9 percent of the passes he threw. No baseball fan expects Derek Jeter to get 10 hits out of 10 at-bats, not even close. Despite a long and successful career, he is unlikely to ever accomplish that feat. Yet, people tend to start each new undertaking with a feeling that nothing less than perfection is acceptable. They are embarrassed deeply by any failure. That is pure nonsense.

As you work to attain a particular objective, wash the word "perfection" out of your brain. Setting an unrealistic standard makes achieving any goal appear to be impossible. Shooting for perfection can lead a person to feel hopeless or possibly undeserving of success. Too many people fail in their endeavors because they measure themselves against perfection. Discouraged, they come to expect defeat and give up. Or, realizing that perfection is out of their reach, they approach the challenge with a fatalistic lack of enthusiasm and effort. Early each semester, a few students will confess to me, "I can never learn all of this material so why should I waste my time trying so hard." Forget perfection (that is an order!). It is neither necessary nor helpful. Perfection and success are not connected. An obsession with being perfect is a stumbling block that limits your chances to succeed.

(2) – *The distance between success and failure is often smaller than you might imagine.* Keep making improvements and you will eventually bridge that gap, possibly sooner than expected. Society frequently places successful people on pedestals as if they have accomplished feats well beyond the reach of mere mortals. In truth, the distance required to move from failure to success is often minute. Do the math; the difference in a .300 batting average in baseball and a .200 batting average is just one additional hit every 3-4 games. Success is within your grasp. In a qualifying round for a recent NASCAR race, the fastest car averaged 196.434 miles per hour and started on the pole position. The 15th fastest car clocked in at 195.495 miles per hours and began the race well back in the pack. Less than one mile per hour separated the 15 fastest cars on the track. In another NASCAR event that took place on the day I wrote this essay, the top 22 cars all finished within 5 seconds of each other. After racing 300 miles (about the distance from Richmond, Virginia, to New York City), the 22nd car was a mere 5 seconds away from first place. The driver lost a considerable amount of money and recognition because of those 5 seconds. A miniscule difference often prevents a person from winning. You might only need to push the odds slightly higher to move into the success column.

(3) – *Improvement is necessary for success and most improvement comes as a direct result of a person's reaction to failure.* When Derek Jeter gets a hit, he is not inclined to make corrections. Why change? His stance at the plate remains the same. He does not consider adjusting his grip on the bat, or the way he watches the baseball, or his

reading of the pitcher's intentions. He is unlikely to spend much time reflecting on performing better. But, 70 percent of his at-bats are failures. He trudges back to the dugout. At those times, Jeter has a golden opportunity. Something clearly went wrong. Maybe he swung the bat too late or got fooled by the movement of the ball. What actually happened? Is some slight adjustment needed? Successful people examine their failures – not to feel guilty or assign blame – but in search of improvement. They do not make excuses; they make corrections. A student once told me that failure was the fertilizer that enables a person to grow toward success. Nothing can improve the odds for success more than a person's reaction to failure. Sure, it hurts. Failure can make people sulk and contemplate quitting. Or, worse, they look for others to fault. Here, at the beginning of this book, rethink your perception of failure. Despite the pain, it is the biggest opportunity you have for improvement.

I mentioned Thomas Edison briefly in the first chapter. He is frequently lauded as the most successful inventor in history. His work ethic was legendary. In his quest to create a functional electric light bulb, Edison experimented tirelessly searching for a usable filament. He tried everything that came to mind, but nothing worked. Time and again, each new possibility flamed out. Eventually, someone asked if so much failure was discouraging. Edison's reply is worth remembering: "I have not failed. I've just found 10,000 ways that won't work." The ability to persevere was surely essential to his ultimate success. On another occasion, he said, "Our greatest weakness lies in giving up. The most certain way to succeed is always to try just one more time." That is a great attitude to develop. It will help you begin to stack the odds for success in your favor. Failure can be a great positive in life rather than a negative but only if it leads to improvement.

A recap of the facets of the Derek Jeter Rule:
(1) – *Perfection is almost never necessary for success.* Rid your mind of the need for perfection. It will only stand in your way.
(2) – *The distance between success and failure is often smaller than you might imagine.* If your efforts are focused on continuously getting better, success is rarely too far away.

(3) – *Improvement is necessary for success and most improvement comes as a direct result of a person's reaction to failure.* When you do not succeed, analyze the experience and learn from it. Make adjustments and be persistent. Failure provides the best opportunity for the essential component of success: improvement.

Success is not a conclusion but rather an ongoing process. The aim of life, as Martin Luther wrote, is "not being but becoming." Envision success as a journey fueled by countless corrections that are each based on a careful examination of mistakes. The emphasis should never be on perfection, but rather the drive to improve and move forward.

Closing Activity: I have confessed here to the problems that the desire for perfection causes in my search for success. Take a moment and consider your own actions. Select one (and only one) personal characteristic that creates a barrier which prevents you from achieving success. Do not identify more because most people can best address only one aspect of their lives at a time. Awareness of a single weakness provides a logical start. Write down several specific actions you can take over the next week to reduce the influence of this negative. The total elimination of a personal flaw might not be possible but, as the push toward success is made, you can monitor and dampen its impact. The questions are simple: What part of you holds you back and what can you do about it? The answers can make the difference between success and failure.

Four: Do You Have Genuine Level 3 Goals?

Person: I want to be a great tennis player.

Suggestion: Go to the court for several hours every day and practice as hard as you can.

Response: I want to be a great tennis player, but I don't want to practice.

**

P: I want to lose weight.

S: Cut out the sugars and starches from your diet.

R: I want to lose weight, but I don't want to quit eating sugars and starches.

**

P: I want to be a better student.

S: Study more hours for your classes and work extra problems each day.

R: I want to be a better student, but I don't want to study hard or spend additional time on problems.

Nothing is unusual or shocking about these conversations. They appear to be the random interactions of day-to-day life, much like a routine played out on a television situation comedy. Although intended to seem a bit humorous, people do think like this. An almost universal characteristic of human inertia lurks behind our inability to act. A body at rest tends to stay at rest. Probably everyone recognizes an element of his or her own personality in Newton's law of physics. When I first began to write *Advanced Accounting* in 1980, an editor told me over coffee, "Every college professor in this country wants to author a textbook, but 95 percent will never write the first word." That is human physics at work in real time. People cling to goals they feel are deeply held, but success is doomed because no work will ever be done, no sacrifice made. The goal will never become a priority and, thus, not a reality.

Why? If people have clear goals, why do they fail to follow up with action?

Former ice hockey superstar Wayne Gretzky is often quoted as saying, "You miss 100% of the shots you don't take." Any discussion of success needs to consider this phenomenon: A goal is set, but no action is ever taken. Do people just become paralyzed? The odds of success obviously fall to zero unless some valid attempt is made at doing the necessary work. I suspect that every person has at least one goal that they think about often but, to quote my mother, "They won't even lift a finger to make it happen." This is not failure. Failure requires the investment of effort. This is an inability to even start.

Why do people sabotage their chance of success in this way? What holds us all back? The path to success is almost never totally hidden. Everyone knows that practice is necessary to become a tennis player or chess master. Diet and exercise lead to weight loss. A good grade in school requires hours of study. If people have identified goals and understand what is required to shift the odds in their favor, why do so many fail to make any legitimate effort?

In striving for success, be honest and evaluate the depth of your desire to achieve each goal. Is the objective real or just a bunch of empty words? *Too often people come to view themselves as failures for not achieving stated goals when, in truth, those goals were no more than fantasies.* A lack of self-awareness about the reality of our desires can lead to personal frustration and a loss of self-esteem. Invariably, early each semester, a few students march into my office to inform me (often in breathless tones) that they want to succeed in my class. I have no reason to dampen their enthusiasm, but they need to be candid with themselves to avoid disappointment. To start that dialogue, I casually ask if their wish for success in my class is a Level-1 goal or a Level-2 goal or a Level-3 goal. They shake their heads in puzzlement. To them, my query seems like some type of strange trick question.

A Level-1 goal is a daydream, a fantasy. It might feel real, but it is not. "I plan to play centerfield for the New York Yankees" is a typical example. Others could include: "I want to be the first explorer to land on Mars," "I want to discover a cure for the common cold," "I want to write plays that are equal to *Hamlet* and *King Lear*." Some students would love an A in my class but only if it came as a gift requiring no work. A Level-1 goal is fun to contemplate, especially when stuck in the mundane existence of daily life, but it is unlikely to become a serious quest. In our hearts, no attempt at success is expected. No inner passion burns to push the dreamer to act. If a baseball scout suddenly appears at my side saying that the Yankees are ready for me if I can just learn to hit a 98 mile per hour fastball, I walk away laughing rather than follow him down the street to the batting cage. People love to revel in their Level-1 dreams. If a genie popped out of a lamp, we would all wish for their automatic delivery. Unfortunately, no matter how hard we protest, serious effort on our part is unlikely to occur.

A Level-2 goal is a desire to be roughly at the average (or maybe within one standard deviation of the average). In that case, "I want to succeed in class" translates into "I would love to make a B, but I am willing to settle for a C." I sometimes refer to Level 2 as a "better than failure" goal. The person is not obsessed with success but certainly does not want to fail. Any outcome above that is a bonus, a reason for rejoicing. The hope is that sufficient interest, work, and energy will be dredged up so that the results are passable and rise to the perceived average range. The effort invested is normally the minimum amount necessary to reach that level of achievement.

A vast majority of our goals in life fall into Level 2. Nothing is wrong with that. When cooking dinner for the family, or learning to play the banjo, or attempting to master the yo-yo or the tango, "I would love to make a B, but I am willing to settle for a C" is the norm on virtually all occasions. No one expects to hit a home run on every attempt at everything. I mowed our grass this afternoon; I was shooting for a C from the start. In life, an occasional A+ is wonderful and exhilarating but probably rare. Several weeks ago, I enrolled in a pottery class to learn about the process of throwing clay and making cups and bowls. I had no interest in becoming a professional potter. The experience was delightful. My abilities seemed to become passable over the weeks in class. During this period, I also attended tai chi classes for exactly the same reason. I wanted to learn the basics about that disciplined moving meditation, but had no intention of developing into a grand master. In both cases, a grade of B would have been nice, but I was happy to take home a C.

Finally, most successful people have a few Level-3 goals that light up their days and nights and push them forward, often at blinding speed. For me, Level-3 goals are an aspect of the human mind that makes existence truly exciting. Without them, daily life begins to feel disappointing and dull. If you feel lost and adrift, you probably need a Level-3 goal.

The presence of two essential characteristics identifies a goal as Level 3.

--First, the degree of difficulty ensures that success is not easy to attain. The challenge must require a personal stretch. People want to be pushed to excel, but need a reason to do the work. Without a worthy goal, no one has sufficient incentive to exert the necessary effort. A great description of this human need is expressed in the movie *A League of Their Own* by the manager (Tom Hanks). In telling one of his players why she should stay with the team and continue to play baseball, Hanks says in no uncertain terms: "It's supposed to be hard. If it wasn't hard, everyone would do it. The hard is what makes it great."

"If it wasn't hard, everyone would do it. The hard is what makes it great." Now that sounds like a true Level-3 goal.

--Second, the desire for success burning within the heart has to be hot enough to push the person to do the difficult work that is necessary. "I want to be strong, but I am not going to exercise" simply means that the goal is not a real priority. It is a dream. A *Level-3 goal verges on obsession.* You can taste the desire when you wake in the morning. You carry it with you through your day and to bed every night. The desire to succeed prods you constantly to use your time well. If you profess the deepest longing to accomplish a specific objective but do not follow up with the needed work, then, by definition, the desire is a Level-1 fantasy and not a Level-3 goal.

Why do people not achieve more success? One of my theories is that we sap our creative energies by mentally dallying too long with Level-1 fantasies. They feel good. They do not demand pain or sacrifice. They are custom-built for procrastination. Consequently, we lack the motivation to seek and develop sufficient Level-3 goals. *Level-1 fantasies expand over time and crowd out Level-3 goals.* Without the desire inherent in Level 3, no work is done and genuine success becomes nearly impossible to achieve. Ask yourself this pointed question:

What difficult challenge do I want to accomplish right now with such intensity that I will begin taking action within the next 24 hours and regularly thereafter?

If no answer pops immediately to mind, you need to extricate yourself from such limited horizons. The odds for success cannot be stacked in your favor without specific goals worthy of the effort. Let me say that again because it is so vitally important: The odds for success cannot be stacked in your favor without specific goals worthy of the effort.

You (yes, YOU) need to start cultivating one or more Level-3 goals. Nothing that I say in these pages could be more relevant to success than that. The writing of this book is one of my Level-3 goals. I hop out of bed at 5:50 each morning ready to start putting words and paragraphs together. I am back at it on Saturday afternoons, Sunday evenings, and at any other free moments. But, that is my Level-3 goal. Your goals need to suit you. What potential accomplishments excite your imagination? Make a list of every possible adventure. Include as many bold projects as possible just to see what grabs your attention. When my children were growing up, they often heard my sermon that "you must generate a lot of ideas before you can ever hope to find a single one that is really good." The business world is always amazed that Apple and Google have such great ideas. My guess is that Apple and

Google simply produce more ideas than other organizations and then have the wisdom to figure out which ones to pursue with a passion.

Pick a goal from your list, try it on, and judge the fit. Does it entice you deeply enough so that you are excited to do the necessary work? Never mistake a Level-1 fantasy for a true Level-3 goal. Level 3 lights a fire. At that point, your energy and effort will come running.

Conceptually, people understand the difference between fantasies and legitimate goals. The difficulty is judging that distinction when looking within, at ourselves. In the movie *Before Sunset*, Julie Delpy's character cuts right to the heart of what I refer to as "goal confusion" when she talks about new leaders who fail to achieve their visions for a better world: "They enjoy the goal, but not the process. But the reality of it is that the true work of improving things is in the little achievements of the day."

Level 1 is only about the dream. Level 3 is a complete process that includes doing the work necessary to succeed.

--Obsessive planning without significant follow up – probably Level 1

--Immediate action – good start toward Level 3

--Continued activity over a period of more than 2-3 days – likely Level 3

--Work nights and weekends to move the process forward – almost certainly Level 3

--Go to bed looking forward to waking up so you can return to the challenge – definitely Level 3

A few years ago, I came upon the best description of a Level-3 experience that I had ever seen, both extremely challenging and personally exciting. My family was vacationing on the Outer Banks of North Carolina. One day we drove to Kitty Hawk to tour the Wright Brothers National Memorial where they first flew their airplane. A major part of the facility was housed in a wonderfully designed exhibition building. Displayed on the inner walls were a number of pertinent quotes from the Wright brothers describing various experiences during their arduous journey to achieve flight. These ruminations were all interesting but one just stunned me. The words rang like they were originating inside my own head. I read and then reread the plaque for several minutes until each word was locked in memory.

"I got more thrill out of flying before I had ever been in the air at all – while lying in bed thinking how exciting it would be to fly."

Orville Wright

Although nothing I have ever done is comparable to building a flying machine by hand, those feelings are still perfectly understandable to me. Often as I chase after a new Level-3 goal, I find myself lying in bed each evening thinking about the thrill of success. Again and again, I picture the moment of achievement. I am not interested in some faraway dream. I want a goal that has immediacy. Work is required right then. And I am willing to do it. In fact, I cannot wait to get started. That, indeed, is a Level-3 goal. *The anticipation of success provides the fuel necessary to get the work done.*

Feel that excitement as much as possible. I have always believed Level-3 clubs should be formed in towns, schools, churches, and other organizations to enable people to share and discuss their goals and the actions being taken to make them come true. The thrill of sharing these dreams aloud with such a supportive group would help to make everyone's success more likely.

Near the beginning of this essay, I posed a question: If people have clear goals, why do they fail to follow up with action? Several times each year, I lead seminars around the country to help college educators become better teachers. Many want to improve, but they are often hesitant about doing the needed work to fulfill that wish. At the beginning of the program, I urge all participants to read "What It Takes to be Great," a marvelously insightful piece in the October 30, 2006, edition of *Fortune* magazine. In subsequent conversations, I draw attention to just two sentences from the article. These few words provide a vision of personal success that I believe everyone should contemplate.

Which group are you in? In many ways, this book boils down to that one question.

From my experience, the *Fortune* magazine quote seems painfully accurate. Over time, most people do stop developing in various aspects of their lives. They become bogged down in Level-1 and Level-2 goals. However, the remaining minority manages to continue to "improve for years and even decades, and go on to greatness." That is what I want. That is what you should want. This ongoing progress is precisely what identifying Level-3 goals can do for you. They provide the purpose and energy to keep pushing you forward. They help you stay located squarely in the group that goes on to greatness. Without Level-3 goals, human tendency is to "stop developing completely."

Closing activity: Identify as many personal goals as possible. Some people have only a few whereas others have scores. Take the time necessary to be complete. Consider every potential accomplishment that is important to you. Then, classify each item on this list as Level 1, Level 2, or Level 3. Remember Level 3 requires a challenge to be faced where a burning desire for success drives you to do the work. Make certain that every project included within Level 3 really does meet that definition. These goals are the ones that serve as beacons for the life you want to live. This is not a list designed for another person. It is solely for you. If they really are genuine Level-3 goals, failure to act will never be a problem.

Five: What Stories Are You Telling Yourself?

For 23 years, I taught CPA exam review programs to thousands of accountants. Almost from the first day, an unusual phenomenon occurred on a regular basis. At the start of every semester, several of the participants would pull me aside to hear their troubled confessions. I felt like a priest being asked to provide absolution. Each looked into my eyes with deep sorrow before beginning their personal litany. "I realize you have helped many people over the years pass the CPA exam, but I'm going to be your first true failure. I cannot pass this test."

At that point, the underlying excuses for such utter hopelessness flowed from their lips. Like the mark on Cain, they each – in their own minds – bore an obvious flaw that blocked all hope of success.

--"I don't do well on standardized tests."

--"I work slowly and can never finish."

--"I get so nervous that I always do poorly on exams."

--"I did not earn good grades in college."

--"I don't have time to study because my spouse is not supportive."

--"I attended a college that was not very good."

--"I am just not smart enough."

--"I have a difficult job and my boss isn't willing to give me any help."

--"I have been out of school for many years and have forgotten most of this stuff."

And on and on. In truth, each of these issues is a legitimate concern for such a difficult examination, but none is insurmountable. Awareness of weaknesses and problems is actually helpful if a person is proactive and takes measures to compensate. But, for these candidates, the concerns had grown out of proportion, into giant roadblocks that made further efforts feel useless. Some element of human nature apparently requires us to view our biggest problem as a huge problem. Inside the head, even minor issues can grow to monumental size.

I was always struck by the number who were absolutely certain of their inability to pass. They had built an entire life story for themselves that invariably ended with failure. Their confessions to me seemed to be designed to soften the blow. "By acknowledging in advance that I have a problem which will prevent me from success, I won't be quite as disappointed when I do fail." Their inadequacy appeared so obvious (to them) that they feared embarrassing themselves by exhibiting any untoward optimism. I suppose imminent failure is not as personally devastating if everyone involved knows that you are well aware that it is on the way.

I have heard that people stuck on high mountain ledges will occasionally jump because the fear of falling becomes so overwhelming. Once again, self-defeat looms as a real obstacle of success.

What an unfortunate way to enter into the exciting challenge of a Level-3 goal. *In a long and arduous journey, attitude is everything.* Confidence is one human characteristic that needs renewing every day. People who expect to fail, do fail. Whether the confessed problems were real or imaginary, these CPA candidates were on the verge of self-inflicted defeat. If failure seems inevitable, no one is ever going to put out the energy necessary to achieve success. Why work hard just to come up short? They were sabotaging their own efforts, reducing the odds for success virtually to zero on that first day.

Everyone carries a view of the world around with them based on personal experiences. Each new day is then interpreted through that filter. Optimism and pessimism are the result, in large part, of our reaction to the past. Perhaps on a math test many years ago, you became confused by one question and did not finish the exam. Although the material was understood, the grade was poor. The incident might have been a pure accident, never to be repeated. By now, it could even have been forgotten. However, the residual feeling that lingers from such experiences can become integrated so thoroughly into the consciousness that it becomes an assumed part of reality. Without being able to recall the reason, you might start confessing: "I have always struggled to finish math tests. I used to like math, but now I avoid those courses because I don't want to fail."

Past events, especially uncomfortable ones, often take on a magnitude of importance well beyond what anyone could have imagined at the time. Our ability to function can become unnecessarily paralyzed, not by outside forces like a former teacher or employer, but by the perceptions of weakness and fear that such encounters leave behind. I am a big fan of the plays of William Shakespeare and no line touches me more deeply than the words of Cassius in *Julius Caesar*:

"The fault, dear Brutus, is not in our stars,
But in ourselves, that we are underlings."

The ability to achieve success is inside each of us, but so is the self-doubt that can drag us toward failure.

In teaching CPA exam review, I always felt that some immediate response to these confessions of inadequacy was required. A more optimistic view had to be offered or these candidates were going to be defeated before getting started. Festering pessimism is never helpful and must be eradicated. I needed to dispel the myth that an affliction made their success impossible. Basically, I had to change the story they were telling themselves. So, I looked each person in the eye and started the work of rebuilding their confidence.

"In all my years as a teacher, I have never yet met anyone who could not be successful on the CPA exam. That includes you. Sure, everyone struggles with issues, but we will work together to overcome those problems. More than anything else, a passing grade requires you to have the intestinal fortitude necessary to do the hard work. And, do it starting right now – not tomorrow, today. Forget failure. It will only scare you into quitting. I never want to hear the word 'failure' from you again. Concentrate on the one thing you can control: making progress right now. Yes, the wall that you face looks impossibly high, but we will conquer it one step at a time. You are scared that the challenge is beyond your ability. That is pure nonsense. People just like you pass the CPA exam every day. If they do it, so can you. We all have weaknesses and issues. But, they can never defeat you unless you let them. The goal is not impossible; it is just difficult. You need to understand the difference. Start today to move forward and you (yes YOU) will get there. Not everyone can arrive at the same time, but if you keep pushing toward the goal, we will be celebrating your success sooner than you expect. This is not a race to see who finishes first. The only thing that matters is that you eventually earn the points necessary to pass. You and I are going to work together to make that happen."

Did this pep talk help? Not always. Some people are so convinced of their inevitable failure that nothing can turn the ship around. However, a great many seemed reassured and most of them did eventually pass. I was always so very pleased when one of the "I can never pass this test" people dropped me a note to say that they had successfully completed all four parts of the test and were licensed as a CPA.

For those people who passed, what changed? This past summer I listened to a fascinating audiobook in my car: *Wild* by Cheryl Strayed. It was long and complex so I will not include a detailed synopsis here. However, at the beginning of this autobiographical work, the author believes that she has lost control over her life (at least in part because of the death of her mother). She decides to focus on a genuine challenge in hopes of regaining inner peace and balance. In that circumstance, I might have taken up a hobby like pottery. With virtually no experience to guide her, Strayed chose to walk 1,100 miles alone through the mountains of California and Oregon on the Pacific Crest Trail. Even now, the level of that challenge seems absurd, beyond belief. Although she faced horribly frightening experiences during those months, she ultimately succeeded. She was not the fastest hiker, actually one of the slowest, but she made it. Along the way, she faced enormous challenges, but figured out ways – often by herself – to get through them all.

One day, I was listening to *Wild* as I drove to campus. The author was getting ready to begin her incredibly long, difficult journey. Not surprisingly, she lost her nerve and almost quit before marching off resolutely to the starting point. In describing her emotions, she wrote a line that is so insightful that I pulled over to the side of the road so I could write it down.

"Fear, to a great extent, is born of a story we tell ourselves."

Shakespeare could not have said it better. "Fear, to a great extent, is born of a story we tell ourselves." For me, this was the most brilliant sentence I read this past year. The words have stuck with me like an arrow for months. And, the sentence is even more relevant if you begin to swap out the word "Fear" for other words such as "Joy," "Excitement," "Hate," "Love," and, of course, "Success."

We all tell ourselves stories each day that hold us back. Look around and you will find dozens.

--I claim to hate roller coasters so I never ride them. The fear is based solely on the story I have told myself since childhood. I have no reason to hate roller coasters and might actually love the thrill. But I stay off of them because that is my story and, apparently, I am sticking with it.

--I tell myself that I do not like the idea of eating snails (or, escargot, in more formal terms). It is a story that I have believed for so long that it seems like an absolute truth. I love oysters, but refuse to touch snails. Why is one more appropriate for me to eat than the other? Perhaps I would enjoy snails just as much as oysters. I am boxed in by the stories I tell myself. My life is limited, not by the stars, but by my own stories.

What stories are you telling yourself about the Level-3 goals that you want to achieve? Are you being held back, not by the difficulty of the challenge, but by the self-doubts that you have allowed yourself to pile up? If the odds of success are going to be stacked in your favor, your own stories cannot block the path. Instead, they should provide the optimism and courage necessary to ensure that you make progress each and every day.

Closing Activity. Pick one of your Level-3 goals where progress has been difficult. You want to make good things happen, but the steps forward have been slow and tentative. Assume that a friend sends an email asking about the success to date on this particular project. Write out a detailed letter describing the actions so far and the results. Give an honest overview of what has occurred, both the advances and the failures.

Wait a few hours and go back and read this letter aloud. Listen carefully to the story being told. Note places where you outline progress. Note descriptions where your words have a positive ring. Likewise, pay attention to negative words and sentences that seem to be merely excuses. What stories are you telling about this Level-3 goal? Then, ask yourself, is it the challenge that is holding you back or the stories you are telling yourself?

Six: One Thought to Write on a Piece of Paper and Tape to Your Wall

Time is the most important weapon you have in your quest to succeed.

Time is more valuable than talent, brains, and strength. Time is like gold: You should hoard and make careful use of it. Invest an infinite amount of time and every challenge can be overcome, every opportunity achieved. But, of course, unlimited time is not available. That is the rub. The week always has 168 hours. Talent, brains, and strength vary from person to person. But, everyone on this planet (whether Bill Gates or Bozo the Clown) has exactly the same number of hours each week. Who succeeds and who fails depends in large measure on how well people manage time. Simply put, those 168 hours can be wasted or made to work for your benefit. With sufficient time, miracles are possible. Although the quantity is rigidly set, what you do with that time is fluid. Absolutely nothing helps stack the odds for success in your favor more effectively than the wise use of every hour, every minute, every single second.

Early each semester (for many years now), I gravely inform my students that I am going to write a magic formula on the board to help them gain the success they seek in my class. Every student immediately jumps to rapt attention because people love to believe that success is wrapped in some kind of mysterious shroud. As in an Indiana Jones movie, if the hidden opening can be uncovered, a secret shortcut will appear to make their lives easier. Slowly, I write on the board:

HOURS EQUAL POINTS

The excitement dies down quickly. Many of the students view my theatrics as a cruel hoax. The secret shortcut is neither a secret nor a shortcut. But, it is the truth. The more time a person works, the more he or she will accomplish. Such advice is not necessarily what any of them wants to hear.

Many people fail to manage time well. They fritter away their hours. Success requires hard work over extended periods, but appealing diversions lurk around every corner to ensnare our attention. Television, movies, beer, the Internet – they all cry out for a piece of that time, often a huge slice. The Bible puts the problem quite succinctly in the book of Matthew: "The spirit is willing but the flesh is weak." Deep in our hearts, we all want to focus on doing whatever work is required for success, but the world teems with distractions and temptations.

Of all the human foibles standing in the way of success, the most treacherous is procrastination. "Play first and work later" is an almost universal litany for the human race. Too often, we never get around to "later." We play first and then play some more. If your motto can become "manage time and avoid procrastination," virtually every challenge becomes doable and doable by you (yes, YOU).

What prevents us from learning to manage our weekly 168 hours better? In truth, until challenges become serious, the development of excellent time management skills is rarely necessary. Whether in school or at work, most people are able to function at an acceptable level without the need to become particularly efficient. Success at common endeavors is not hard to achieve. People squander time, but still get by. If you want to become the average driver, or the average cook, or the average swimmer, or the average college student, the challenge is not overwhelming for most people. As a result, we all acquire bad habits. Frittering away the hours is a pleasant pastime learned well in youth and carried into adult lives. Technology in the form of Facebook, Twitter, Pinterest, and Instagram steals our moments while we are distracted. Mediocrity develops into a personal standard. Only when we encounter a challenge that pushes us beyond our comfort zone does the effective use of time become vital. We hit a wall where previous strategies no longer suffice.

If you learn from the experience, that wall is a wonderful aid to development. Such a challenge can have a positive impact on the rest of life, enabling you to grow into a stronger person. However, reaction to that wall is entirely up to you. I believe strongly in personal evolution. I preach that to my students. I work to practice that in my own life. People are capable of growth. You can learn to become more efficient. The past is not a trap unless you acquiesce. Sloppy time management habits do not form a nasty tattoo that you must live with for the rest of your life. Evolution enables everyone to make the improvements that are necessary for success. Facing each challenge is like readying for a new battle. You need to reassess former tactics. Can they still bring success or must adjustments be made?

Frequently, struggling students look at me with resignation in their eyes and state with absolute assuredness, "That is just the way I am." My response never varies: "That is absolute, utter nonsense. If you are not dead, opportunities arise every day that allow change and growth. Start by learning to make better use of time and you will immediately improve your chances to succeed. Experiment with adjustments in strategy and then assess how each works. Adjust, assess, adjust, assess. That takes time, but the process will move you toward improvement and the goal you seek." Exert control over time to gain improvement and the odds of success will move in your favor.

In military discussions, one of the most famous sayings is that "generals are always fighting the previous war." Military leaders can be criticized for looking back at the level of success achieved by the use of earlier maneuvers. The claim is that they tend to rely too heavily on past lessons as they charge forward into future conflicts. They are trapped by history. If a cavalry operation was decisive in the last operation, more horses will be requested for upcoming warfare even if the enemy is now ensconced in a metal tank. Our ability to adapt becomes weakened when we become too enamored of lessons already learned.

You are not a captive of the past. Michael Jordan, the basketball legend has said: "If you run into a wall, don't turn around and give up. Figure out how to climb it, go through it, or work around it."

Increasingly difficult challenges require better time management tactics. Just because a strategy has worked previously does not mean it will continue to succeed when a more complex problem appears on the horizon. That is where growth occurs. You have 168 hours each week. Be ready to evolve and change the use of those hours either before, or after, you run up against each new wall.

Good advice, like a good friend, sticks with you for a long time. Forty years ago, I read a marvelous book titled *Up the Organization* by Robert Townsend. This ingenious little work was filled with lesson after lesson of common sense advice on helping business leaders become more effective primarily by getting the best from their people. I was astounded. Townsend put into clear words what seemed practically self-evident. Specifically, a few words about his approach to time management have influenced me virtually every day over the past four decades:

> "It isn't easy to concentrate. I used to keep a sign opposite my desk where I couldn't miss it if I were on the telephone (about to make an appointment) or in a meeting in my office: 'Is what I'm doing or about to do getting us closer to our objective?' That sign saved me from a lot of useless trips, lunch dates, conferences, junkets, and meetings."

"Is what I'm doing or about to do getting me closer to my objective?" When you get to the point where that question is always considered, you have taken a giant step in managing time. Gradually, the odds of success will begin to swing in your favor.

Closing Activity: Think back over the past day. Identify one task where you made especially good use of available time. Perhaps, it was shopping for groceries, learning to work with a new phone, or practicing the guitar. Why were these moments so effective? Answering this question draws attention to your capacity for making good use of time. Success breeds success, so keeping track of efficient time management helps replicate such moments in the future.

Then, while still considering the many activities of the past 24 hour period, estimate the total amount of time wasted. Think about the number of minutes and hours that, in your mind, were not well used. In modern society, complaints about lack of time have become epidemic. This mindset alone can overwhelm our efforts. It provides a universal excuse for failure. Careful scrutiny might be necessary to find it, but the sheer volume of time at your disposal is likely to be significant. Although everyone is incredibly busy, most people have the time needed to change their lives if they merely cut down on their inefficiencies.

Seven: My Own Personal Wall

Okay, where are we? From my perspective, a summation of our progress to date should include:

--Perfection is not necessary for success, so forget about it.

--Success is likely to be closer than you imagine. The gap will be bridged if you continue to improve.

--Improvement is most likely gained through the careful analysis of failures.

--True Level-3 goals are necessary and should not be crowded out by Level-1 fantasies.

--Because the available number of hours each week is set, efficient time management is essential.

--Personal evolution results as previous strategies are adapted to meet more complex challenges.

--Make certain that the stories you tell yourself have a positive, rather than negative, impact.

There are relatively few words here, but they provide essential advice for stacking the odds of success in your favor.

Sounds good, but anyone can hand out advice. That is the easy part. The world is filled with advice, but not with success. Businesses often hire consultants who charge enormous fees for the sage advice they render. The joke is that such consultants often provide costly expertise on matters where they have no personal experience. Without breaking a sweat, I can describe how to become the next Michelangelo, Albert Einstein, or William Shakespeare. Providing advice is simple. Doing the actual work necessary to emulate such successful individuals is the true challenge.

During the American Civil War, soldiers on both sides wrote home describing two types of generals. One led from the rear where he could remain safe, but never knew precisely what was happening at the battlefront. The other led from the trenches where he risked death, but worked with timely and firsthand information. Not surprisingly, the soldiers honored the latter and mocked the former.

I have no interest in serving as a consultant or a general who shies away from the conflict. Direct and personal insight is essential for evolutionary growth. Consequently, I want to share my own experience of facing an overwhelming challenge where I successfully managed to stack the odds in my favor.

People never know in advance what wall they will hit that changes their life. In hindsight, I do know the wall that altered mine. The encounter took place during the spring of 1970, and culminated on May 6-8 of that year. Long decades have now passed, but the experience still influences how I face each of life's new challenges. Hitting the wall and successfully pushing through the challenge has been one of the most positive experiences of my life. I discovered the power of personal evolution. I learned to manage my time effectively and gained confidence in myself. If you (yes, YOU) plan to stack the odds for success in your favor, such lessons are essential.

Having majored in accounting during college, I took the CPA examination in a hotel ballroom in Charlotte, North Carolina, on May 6, 7, and 8 of 1970. At that time, this comprehensive set of tests was 19 ½ hours long and was only given each May and November. Then, and now, a candidate had to pass all four of the individual sections as one of the requirements for admission into the accounting profession. At that time, the pass rate on each separate test was roughly 33 percent. That percentage is eye-catching because it reflects the true intensity of the challenge. The percentage of candidates who pass is now somewhat higher but, in those years, two of every three candidates walked out of each of the four tests with a failing grade. Not surprisingly, the pressure was mind numbing. Failure meant an additional six months of study before the next set of exams was given with their own 33 percent pass rate. Given the odds, many bright, hard-working accountants took the CPA exam for years without ever achieving success. Most faced the challenge with a genuine sense of dread.

I returned to college after my Christmas vacation in January 1970, a senior accounting major with decent grades earned at a good school. A job waited for me following graduation. I had a fiancée and wedding plans. I was ready (at least I believed) for adult life. But, the CPA examination stood in my path – very much like a giant wall. In 1970, little information was disclosed publicly about those four tests. Afterwards, I likened the experience to childbirth in the Victorian Era. Candidates were mostly left in the dark about the entire process until arriving at the testing site. Then, they had to figure out what they were supposed to do as they went along. Hand-holding was not available. Today, many large review programs are in the business of explaining each step to help candidates pass. Plus, an extensive website provides more information than anyone could possibly want about every aspect of the CPA exam. In 1970, almost none of that was available.

Passing was important to me. I wanted to get on with life. I was ready to be an adult and stop having to sit in little desks, listen to lectures, and take tests. Moreover, I had a burning desire to pass all four parts on my first attempt. In college, my grades were fairly good, but far from stellar. For many reasons, the elevated level of ambition that I felt so intensely in high school had disappeared. I missed the feeling. An essential part of me had gotten misplaced during those four years. The CPA exam offered the chance to recapture the internal drive that had pushed me to succeed. I was not aware at the time, but completion of this examination became a genuine Level-3 goal for me.

I had attended a small high school where the teachers seemed to care about my well-being and progress. Within that nurturing environment, I graduated number one in my class. I then enrolled at a well-known research university where professors appeared 100 times more interested in their own studies than they did in mine. Occasionally, I felt like an annoyance to them rather than like a human being. As a newly minted freshman, I quickly decided that becoming one of the top students was not my destiny and so, without much reflection or fight, settled in to being an average college student. *Mediocrity is a disease that is easy to catch.*

Success on the CPA exam offered a chance for redemption. I wanted to pass all four sections immediately to reignite the element of my personality that I had allowed college to dampen down: my passion for success. (Not coincidentally, I later became a teacher, in part, because I wanted future college students to have a better educational experience than my own.) To ready myself for the battle, during January 1970, I read every piece of available information describing the CPA exam and the best method of preparation. Most articles vaguely suggested that candidates learn everything included in the courses taken in college covering accounting, taxes, auditing, business law, and the like. "Learn everything" is a tough starting spot for any challenge. February 1 was scheduled as my first day of preparation. That morning, I opened a textbook and set out on my journey to find success. Somewhat like Christopher Columbus, I plunged into the unknown.

Three days later, I realized that I had slammed into a wall. I had made a huge miscalculation. All of the possible topics encompassed too much highly complicated material. The information could not be absorbed fast enough. I was already overwhelmed. The brutal truth was that I had no idea how to pass the May 1970 CPA exam. And, time was slipping away quickly. I yearned for success, but did not know how to achieve it at that level. During high school and college, I had followed the conventional "cramming" approach of writing down extensive class notes and highlighting book passages. Key words and ideas were then memorized to be regurgitated on a test every few weeks. Most of those examinations covered only two or three chapters of material. By paying close attention to the teacher, test questions could even be anticipated. Almost immediately, I realized my previous preparation strategy was inadequate. The CPA exam was too big. In simple terms, I had always prepared for a 100-yard dash, but now faced a marathon. I had to adapt immediately, or I was going to fail.

The previous essay included Michael Jordan's exhortation on encountering a challenge. Those feel-good words were invigorating, hopeful: "If you run into a wall, don't turn around and give up. Figure out how to climb it, go through it, or work around it." Unfortunately, such ethereal advice does not always translate into an action plan when the reality of a massive wall looms in your path. I was in a panic, banging my head repeatedly against a wall that seemed much too big for my meager abilities. At that moment, a specific response rather than a clever motto was urgently required. What does "climb it" or "go through it" mean in real life?

Too many people latch onto encouraging phrases as if words alone provide the keys to great achievement. *Words that do not lead to positive action are useless.*

Realizing that success was in serious jeopardy, I sat at my desk one afternoon in early February and listed all of the relevant facts as I knew them. When facing a difficult challenge, writing down the factual information is a helpful starting point for a revised strategy. This exercise provides a structure for planning. Too often, we allow the facts of a situation to remain nebulous, vague and cluttered thoughts floating around in the back of our brains. On paper, they take on a physical form that can suggest reasonable actions. Rather than growing to an impossible size and scope inside our minds, the problem starts to become finite and, hence, manageable. An active imagination can turn the simplest challenge into an impassable mountain.

- Fact One: The minimum passing grade on each section of the CPA exam was – and still is – 75. By that time, I had absolutely no interest in making one point higher than necessary. Special awards are handed out for truly outstanding scores. Achieving such recognition did not even cross my mind. For once in my life, perfection was not an obsession. I wanted four grades of 75. I needed 75 points on each exam and nothing more. *To succeed at a challenge, you need to have specific goals in mind.* A vague target is much harder to hit than one that is well-drawn. I often tell my students, "If you don't know where you want to go, a roadmap is not going to be any help." I knew my goal: 75.

- Fact Two: In grappling with a difficult challenge, no one can win every battle. But, that is not crucial. Victory in the war is the objective. Priorities must be identified along the way. Compromises become necessary. I could study for my classes at college or prepare for the CPA exam. Not enough time was available to do well on both. That afternoon, I decided that the CPA exam was my primary goal. In my heart, I longed to get through that particular wall. But, I also needed to be honest with myself. I was not ready to sacrifice my grade point average entirely. Those class grades would become important if I ever chose to apply to a graduate program or law school. Although the study time for my college classes had to be reduced, I was only willing to let my semester GPA drop by a half-point. If a 3.6 average seemed possible, I would accept an average as low as 3.1 if the extra time gave me a legitimate shot at passing the CPA exam. That was a conscious decision. *Never be naïve; success requires sacrifice. Before beginning the journey, determine the level of sacrifice you are willing to accept and be certain you can deal with those results. Being unhappy with the sacrifice ruins the thrill of success.*

- Fact Three: The real issue, though, was the effectiveness of my time management. That was obvious. I still had sufficient opportunity for study: 168 hours every week. If HOURS EQUAL POINTS as I have long claimed, more of that time had to be devoted to my preparation and the maximum number of points earned during each hour. I needed more hours and more efficiency. To propel myself into the upper 33 percent of all exam candidates, I had to have better time management skills. *When a challenge begins to get the best of you, stop and rethink your use of time.*

My priorities were set. I understood the level of sacrifice I was willing to make. Now, success depended on improved time efficiency. Radical changes in my approach were necessary. Merely saying that I wanted to make 75 was not sufficient. I could chant that number all day, every day, and not add a single point. I could meditate about the goal; I could pray over it. But, real action was required. Focusing on a desired outcome is always easier than doing the work needed to move from here to there. My preparation had to evolve in order to stack the odds of making 75 in my favor. Immediate change was mandatory. Further procrastination was not an option. I identified five specific adjustments and started that same day to implement them.

1 – To this day, I tend to go to bed and rise each morning at very specific times. At heart, I am an accountant who prefers to live a fairly regimented life. My first adjustment was to stay up 30 extra minutes each night and wake 30 minutes earlier the following day for additional study. A full hour was immediately added to my daily routine, a huge increase in available time. For three months, I could learn to live on a reduced level of sleep. My body would just have to adapt to this new schedule. *When facing a difficult challenge, be willing to push yourself beyond your comfort zone.* "Always dream and shoot higher than you know you can do. Don't bother just to be better than your contemporaries or predecessors. Try to be better than yourself." Those words from William Faulkner say more about the challenge of stretching yourself to achieve greatness than anything else I have ever read.

"Try to be better than yourself" is a goal well worth pursuing.

At the close of each day, I climbed into bed at the regular time, but then continued to work on the CPA exam for another 30 minutes (no matter how tired I felt) before turning off the light. In hopes of easing the psychological burden, I told myself that I was getting rest while still studying. My alarm was set to ring a half-hour earlier. Upon waking the next morning, I reopened the textbook and went back to studying while still lying in bed. My daily level of coverage increased markedly and that felt good. I quickly found that starting each day having already completed a measurable amount of work was motivating. "I knocked out 30 extra minutes this morning even before getting out of bed" was a theme that ran repeatedly through my head during those weeks. Never underestimate the importance of maintaining a positive mindset. Exercise every possible trick to keep the confidence level high. Long hours of work are so much easier if you feel upbeat about the progress being made. The work was never great fun, but having a Level-3 goal made it much better.

2 – The difficulty of finding more time to study was not the only barrier to success. I needed an efficient methodology to accumulate and organize such a massive amount of information. Today, I might have downloaded an app for my smartphone. With no such advanced technology available, I relied on a large package of 3 X 5 cards. In the past, I would have covered those cards with thousands of words to memorize. A better solution was needed for this challenge. It took too long and created too much data. My notes had to be boiled down to the essential terms, formulas, and processes that had not yet been mastered. When I encountered any new information while studying, I penciled a related question on one side of a card with the answer on the back. Most importantly, I kept every response to 10 or fewer words. I put a strict limit on the amount of knowledge needed for success. If I could not reduce an answer to about 10 words, I broke the question into smaller parts. Or, I simply chose to ignore the information and tossed the card aside. My grade only needed to be 75, not 100. When perfection is eliminated as an issue, smart choices are easier to make. *Narrow down the challenge; do not allow it to grow to an infinite size.*

3 – From that day forward, the growing pack of 3 X 5 cards went with me everywhere. If a spare second became available, I pulled those cards out, read a question, constructed an answer in my mind, and then turned the card over to see if my knowledge was sound. *Every free moment in life is a golden opportunity for improvement, but only if you are ready to seize it.* I rode the bus between campuses, reading cards. I sat in classrooms waiting for the teacher, reading cards. I washed my clothes at the local laundromat, reading cards. As a challenge grows more daunting, preparation must become more methodical. I stopped eating meals with my friends. Instead, I sat alone with my food and those cards. Three meals per day at 30 minutes each is an added 90 minutes of daily study time, an increase of more than 10 hours per week. Unless a person is prepared to make use of available time, it will be wasted.

I recently visited the Picasso Museum in Barcelona. On display were a few of the notebooks that Picasso carried with him throughout his youth so that he could sketch people, hands, dogs, noses, and the like just for practice. If continuous improvement is a key to achieving success, then a person must always be prepared to make excellent use of free moments.

4 – I had a long conversation with my fiancée (now my wife of over 43 years). She attended college an hour from my school. I explained the importance to me of passing the CPA exam and its impact on my future career and our lives together. She was so willing to be supportive. We agreed to only see each other one day a week until after the exam. During part of every date, she would ask me questions from those 3 X 5 cards and check my answers on the back. *The more difficult the challenge, the more important a support group becomes.* We are all capable of scaling tall mountains by ourselves, but the odds for success increase dramatically with the help of friends and family. Most people are delighted to be of assistance if you talk with them honestly about what you are trying to accomplish and why. All of life works better with open and clear communications. Always let others know that they are needed and how they can help. An adequate level of communication solves a great many problems.

5 – My final adjustment was the one that I continue to believe was most critical. And, with sufficient motivation, it was easy. Each night I meticulously wrote out a schedule for every minute of the coming day. That list was always in my pocket and I followed it as closely as possible, often obsessively. For example, from 9 a.m. until 10, I might plan to study statistical sampling. From 10 a.m. until 11:15, perhaps I attended class. From 11:15 a.m. until noon, I ate lunch and read through my cards. During those three months, not a single day began with any uncertainty. Reducing uncertainty is essential for effective time management and, hence, achieving success. As soon as my eyes opened in the morning, I knew what needed to be done and when. Each minute was detailed on the list in my pocket. *Organize every day in advance and then have the discipline to stick with that schedule.* Too often, we get to the end of a long day and wonder how so much time managed to slip away. That is no way to conquer a difficult challenge. I set my schedule every evening for those three months and stuck with it.

-- *When facing a difficult challenge, be willing to push yourself beyond your comfort zone.*

-- *Narrow down the challenge; do not allow it to grow to an infinite size.*

-- *Every free moment in life is a golden opportunity for improvement, but only if you are ready to seize it.*

-- *The more difficult the challenge, the more important a support group becomes.*

-- *Organize every day in advance and then have the discipline to stick with that schedule.*

Today, as I write these words, my CPA exam efforts seem a bit fanatical. But, at that time, the magnitude of the challenge appeared almost beyond comprehension. I wanted success. I needed success. I had to find a way to stack the odds in my favor.

In the first week of August 1970, a registered letter arrived at my parent's house informing me that I had passed all four parts of the CPA exam. My fiancée (actually my wife by that time) and I whooped and hollered and danced around the room. Two of the grades were 75s, but the other two were 81s. We laughed about studying too hard, but we had made it through the wall. Success is virtually always a team effort.

Failure seemed inevitable in February. But I stopped, changed my strategy in order to make these five adjustments, and shifted the odds in my favor. As Robert Frost writes in one of his lovely poems, "that has made all the difference."

Closing Activity: Practice is ever so helpful. It changes the theoretical to the real. Take out a sheet of paper and create a schedule of what you hope to accomplish over the next 24 hours. Include meals, work, exercise, rest, and anything else you want to do. Make the listing reasonably detailed including specific activities and times. Be optimistic; challenge yourself to achieve great things. Start with the question: "If tomorrow is an absolutely perfect day in my quest for success, what should happen and when?" Carry the schedule with you at all times. Have the discipline to follow it to the letter. At the end of 24 hours, assess the results. Did scheduling help you accomplish more than normal? How difficult was it to create and follow? What tweaks should you make to accomplish more the next day? Remember that the goal is to eliminate uncertainty involving the use of time. All essential decisions about the use of time are determined in advance.

Of course, scheduling out each new day is nothing that started with me. In the book *Wolf Hall*, author Hilary Mantel has her protagonist Thomas Cromwell (in the court of Henry VIII) saying in roughly the year 1535, "It's all very well planning what you will do in six months, what you will do in a year, but it's no good at all if you don't have a plan for tomorrow." Those are my sentiments exactly.

Eight: Monitor and Reassess – Addressing the Ebenezer Scrooge Question

"What do you want to be when you grow up?" The question is often asked of small children as a way to engage them in conversation or gain an understanding of their personal interests. No one expects any particular answer to be a final choice. Their opinions are likely to be different almost every day. As they turn into teenagers, young people usually contemplate a wide range of possibilities. Initial aspirations provide direction, but interests often change radically as a person matures. At 14, a girl who dreams of becoming a writer keeps a detailed diary. A 16-year old boy who hopes to own a restaurant cooks an occasional dinner for his family. Despite those early starts, eventual careers might well have nothing to do with writing or food service. Neither friends nor family should be shocked or upset by that outcome. The answer to the question "what do you want to be?" can change quickly.

We expect adults to have a clearer understanding of the proper course for their lives. For example, we skewer politicians for changing their minds on any issue, branding them with the incriminating label of "flip-flopper." We view any altered opinion as a sign of weakness, an indication that the person was either mistaken or not deeply committed to the original course of action. We do not judge either of those excuses favorably. "I've made up my mind so don't confuse me with the facts," is humorous only because the sentiment reflects reality in much of our society. It is a safe strategy.

Everyone knows that adult decisions have consequences that are usually much more serious than those of children. This observation is hardly radical or new. The words of Paul, found in the New Testament, have been quoted countless times over the past 2,000 years: "When I was a child, I spoke like a child, I thought like a child, I reasoned like a child. When I became a man, I gave up childish ways." However, that does not mean that every adult choice must be permanent.

In truth, we adults need to consider the wisdom of the path we follow, at least pondering the question now and then. Over the course of a lifetime, our hopes, desires, and interests never stop evolving. Level-3 goals are essential; they provide guidance and inject energy and excitement into life. But they are rarely cast in stone. If a tennis ball is thrown from the top of the Empire State Building, you can watch its slow, steady descent and there is not one thing you can do to alter the result. Thankfully, most of life is different. Every new day offers a chance to reconsider and change directions. *Never waste today's energy chasing yesterday's goals.* We should reassess professed objectives on an ongoing basis. Even the truest of Level-3 goals can gradually morph into a mere fantasy. The metamorphosis is easy to overlook without vigilant attention. Over time, people can fall into a rut and continue to push blindly forward toward some outdated goal even if that path now threatens to head them over a cliff.

What then is the adult parallel to "What do you want to be when you grow up?"

In Charles Dickens's classic story *A Christmas Carol*, Ebenezer Scrooge spends all of his time and energy in a quest to gain as much wealth as possible. That Level-3 goal is a burning desire that he works day and night to achieve. He never even considers an alternative. As the tale begins, reassessment is long overdue.

On Christmas Eve, the Ghost of Christmas Yet to Come pays a visit. Scrooge is escorted to a mysterious location where he is presented with a frightening vision of the future: his own grave and the unsympathetic reaction of relatives and acquaintances to the news of his death. It is a brutal experience. The question posed by this scene is obvious although unasked:

Here is where your current efforts are heading.
Is this the ending you really want?

I refer to this as the Ebenezer Scrooge Question, one we should all consider on a regular basis. When framed in this way, the miser's answer is a resounding "No!" The previous Level-3 goal of hoarding money is abandoned immediately as a result of this new perspective. Scrooge wakes the next morning as a different, and better, person. Rather than continuing to charge ahead to a conclusion he no longer wants, new Level-3 goals are adopted. He alters the way he lives and treats people. He now has a different philosophy. Was Ebenezer Scrooge a flip-flopper? Is this change a sign of weakness? Of course not. Previous goals were rightfully reassessed as his opinions matured.

Before that fateful night, Scrooge had a well-defined objective. He understood the effort required to attain success and willingly did it. The process worked efficiently as he moved ever closer to the riches he desired. What was the problem? Why do we celebrate his change? Scrooge was forced to consider where his actions were heading and did not like the expected outcome. On the path of life, reassessment is both permitted and encouraged. True success is only possible with correct goals.

Scrooge was lucky to have outside intervention from the spirit world. A peek into the future led to a fundamental improvement in his Level-3 goals. Unfortunately, ghosts are not very dependable. They rarely appear among us to provide such helpful guidance. Without other-world assistance, how do you manage to address the basic question: Here is where current efforts are heading; is this the ending you want? Or, perhaps, a more jarring version of this inquiry serves as a better call to action:

What will others write on your tombstone and will you be satisfied with those words?

The finality of these questions puts the evaluation of our current goals into perspective.

Unless spirits start appearing on a regular basis to serve as a prompt, an Ebenezer Scrooge Day should be scheduled formally once or twice every year. On that date, each person reconsiders the continued relevance of all Level-3 goals. Set a specific day for reassessment because nothing happens by accident. Have an honest conversation with yourself about where you are going and why. Plan to focus on the direction of current efforts and the continued desirability of the anticipated result. When you eventually arrive at the final destination, success needs to feel like success.

Even with planning, reassessment can still happen at odd moments. After teaching in college for over four decades, occasional accolades are likely. Such awards are always gratifying. But, recognition can be a trap because, almost without exception, it is based on a perception of previous accomplishments. As investment commercials are required to say, "Past performance is no guarantee of future results." This disclaimer should never be ignored. Never rest on your laurels. In teaching and, I suppose, virtually all other aspects of life, a person is only as good as he or she is today. The students who sit in my class are not the least bit interested in whether I was a good teacher last year. They only want to know whether I am going to be a good teacher today. Some people linger in the past while others long for the future. Success *always dwells in the current moment*. The question to be addressed is the same every new day. You see where this is heading. Is this the ending you really want?

Although I tend to discount honors, one awards ceremony has helped me make a reassessment of my role as a college professor. Each spring, at the Robins School of Business at the University of Richmond (where I teach), a senior recognition dinner is held. As is typical of such events, a number of awards are presented to students and faculty, some serious but many humorous. A few years ago, I was in attendance sitting with a group of students when an upcoming honor was announced: Scariest Professor in the Business School. Immediately, every student sitting nearby turned and pointed at me. I am bald and nearsighted. At 5' 8" and 155 pounds, I am hardly a vision of Freddy Krueger. But, the envelope was opened and my name was called. That is truly an odd feeling.

Those students were on the cusp of graduation. I had worked closely with many of them for several years. Apparently, that is how I was to be remembered. In a room of 200, I was the most frightening person. Given the opportunity, they would have carved "Scariest Professor" on my tombstone. I did not immediately embrace the epitaph.

A few minutes later, the final award of the evening was announced: "The Professor Who Cares the Most." I won that honor also. Driving home that night, an Ebenezer Scrooge image of my own tombstone appeared before me with the engraving: "The scariest professor who cared the most." It was a truly interesting mental picture. After a bit of reflection, I decided that this vision of my future suited me just fine. At least for the teaching part of my life, I liked where I was heading. As far as I was concerned, those words could be carved over my grave. I had no objection. Since that time, I have worked hard to burnish both reputations – scary and caring. Not one or the other – but both. They have now merged in my mind to form a serious Level-3 goal: I want to remain the scariest professor who cares the most.

Stop and think about all the roles you play each day: worker, student, spouse, parent, boss, child, neighbor, and friend. You probably have different Level-3 goals for each segment of your life. The goal for a marriage is necessarily different from the goal for a job. Take a moment to reassess each Level-3 goal. Based on current efforts, where are you headed? Assume that the people who know you best were asked to create an award to be etched into your tombstone after death. What would you expect it to say?

-- "Nicest guy in the world"
-- "Best television watcher"
-- "Always a follower"
-- "Rarely used talents wisely"
-- "Out of the box thinker"
-- "Ambitious and innovative"
-- "Needed to be pushed"
-- "Dependable and hardworking"

For each Level-3 goal, try to anticipate what the people involved would say about you? Does that please you as a final epitaph? If not, then, like Scrooge, it is time to make serious changes.

Closing Activity: How can you create the environment of an Ebenezer Scrooge Day? Start by selecting your most important Level-3 goal. Pick the one that calls to you the most deeply. Now assume that a local television station has decided to produce a short program on your quest for success. A reporter and camera crew are dispatched to follow around as you work toward achieving this goal. They videotape your actions, conversations, and meetings for a couple of days. They talk with others about you, your talents, and achievements. As their last activity, they ask you in an interview to describe how you are going to feel when you successfully complete this specific goal. Picture yourself looking into the camera and consider what you would say. Are you satisfied with that answer?

Next, assume that a few weeks later the completed show appears on the nightly news. It is all about you and your quest. The reporter starts the segment with an opening sentence or two to explain your goal to the audience and what has been observed as you work toward it.

--What would you like for this reporter to say about you and your work ethic as you strive to reach this goal? How do you want to be remembered by those who have observed you in action?
--What do you think the reporter would be most likely to say? What is an honest appraisal? After following you around for days and talking with other people about your efforts, what impression is most likely?

Ultimately, the questions you want to address are: Where are my current efforts heading? Is that the ending that I really want?

Or, in a slightly different way: What will others write on my tombstone? Will I be satisfied with those words?

Nine: Feel the Ball in Your Hands

The image is easily recognizable on the television screen, broadcast in high definition so the audience feels right in the midst of the action. Mere seconds remain in the championship basketball game. A player has been fouled and stands alone at the free throw line waiting to take the shot that will spell the difference between winning and almost winning. After months of hard work, the season falls squarely on this one set of shoulders. For that moment, nothing else matters. Thousands in the stands and millions at home lean forward in anticipation. The tension seems unbearable. The ball is placed in the player's hands, the knees bend, and the shot flies perfectly to the target. Victory! The shooter is mobbed by teammates and fans. Success never feels more alive than in those magical moments.

As the excitement plays out, the announcers provide almost pre-scripted adulations to describe the newly crowned star.
--"What incredible talent. Made the final shot look easy."
--"Probably stood in the back-yard as a kid practicing free throws hundreds of times."

Maybe so. *But, a lot more goes into a winning performance than mere talent and physical repetition.* Do not be naïve. Nothing is ever that simple. Players must be mentally ready to succeed if they hope to hit the winning shot. Although hours of practice on the court are essential, the mind also has to be properly trained. In the sports world, one of the most accepted axioms is that "the will to win is important, but the will to prepare is vital." We too often consider only the physical side of that admonition—lifting weights, running laps, and the like. Never underestimate the need for mental training and discipline. To stack the odds of success in our favor, a strong mind is as important as a strong body, a requirement that applies to the world outside of sports as much as it does to the world inside. For Level-3 goals, the gap between success and failure can best be bridged by excellent overall preparation (both mental and physical).

Few of us will ever need to sink one shot to win a championship, but we frequently face critical moments when an important outcome hangs in the balance. In such endeavors, that is the point where success happens. Because I am a verbal person willing to express my opinions, I receive invitations to deliver speeches a few times each year. Occasionally, I find myself in front of a large audience faced with the very immediate challenge of filling the room with words and sentences that are both interesting and thoughtful. Although exhilarating, the experience is always edged with tension. From the first word, every presentation teeters precariously between success and failure. To succeed, mental preparation is absolutely vital. As in basketball, talent and physical repetition by themselves are not adequate.

When the time comes to speak, I walk to the podium and set my notes aside, safely out of the way. I then step around to the front of the stage so that I can talk directly with the individuals in attendance. At that moment, one thought is laser-focused in my brain: If I am able to carry on long discussions in my office without a carefully typed script, addressing a room full of people should be just as easy. Speaking to many is no different than talking with one. That is a considered part of my mental preparation. A speech is simply a conversation where I happen to do all the talking. (If interested, one of my speeches is available for viewing by searching for "Joe Hoyle Last Lecture" at YouTube.com. Among a variety of topics, I talk further about the William Faulkner and Michael Jordan quotes mentioned previously in these writings.)

People in attendance at these programs often express surprise that I abandon prepared remarks and just chat with the group in a casual manner. At the conclusion, audience members frequently approach to ask how I manage to deliver an entire speech without being chained to extensive notes. Having the appropriate mindset is my essential first step, but I also rely on a preparatory technique—one that has helped me to stack the odds of success in my favor during many endeavors over the decades. In advance of an activity, I work to mentally visualize success. I believe this practice has made me a more successful person. Whether sinking the game winning shot, delivering a speech to hundreds, or facing similar tasks, visualization can also help you (yes, YOU).

Throughout life, seemingly inconsequential events have long-lasting effects. In 1973, at the urging of an aunt, I read a book with the odd title *Psycho-cybernetics*. I believed I was doing no more than humoring a favorite relative. In reality, my approach to many of life's toughest challenges was forever altered. Today, the term "psycho-cybernetics" sounds like a horror movie involving a deranged robot. But this book's simple message is that people can train themselves to become more successful.

The author, Maxwell Maltz, starts with the logical premise that humans learn best through practice. That is hardly a startling revelation. As an illustration, consider the sequential steps required in learning to drive a car. The student slides in behind the steering wheel and turns the ignition key. The driver puts the car into the proper gear and applies pressure to the gas pedal. The driver steers the car through the street, paying careful attention to highway signs, oncoming vehicles, and pedestrians. With sufficient repetition, virtually every new driver achieves a reasonable level of mastery. Such routines can be followed to gain a wide variety of skills from ice skating to cake baking.

"Practice makes perfect" is a cliché, but that label does not reduce the truth it conveys.

Maltz asserts that anyone can achieve significant benefits by practicing tasks mentally, visualizing the successful performance of every activity. He instructs readers to use their minds to replicate each individual step in a process that is functioning with perfection. Imagine putting the car into gear and accelerating as you begin to steer out into traffic and down the street. How does the operation feel when it goes well? The term "mental imagery" is now commonly applied to this type of exercise. According to Maltz, visualization provides many of the same improvements as physical practice. And, it is quicker and more convenient. A student can mentally drive an automobile every waking moment anticipating the proper responses to a plethora of potential hazards. Or, a basketball player is able to visualize sinking foul shot after foul shot while relaxing each evening.

If you want to become an outstanding golfer and it rains one day, the opportunity for practice on the course is lost. Maltz would likely suggest sitting in a chair at home, mentally feeling the golf club in your hands and the grass under foot. Think about seeing the ball lying on the ground. Look at it carefully. Notice the dimples embedded in its surface. Feel the club moving back and then forward in a smooth, even swing as your body follows through with correct alignment. Hear the club head hit the ball and mentally see it fly off in a perfectly straight arc. Break up the entire process into as many separate components as possible and visualize each being carried out in proper fashion. The vision must be as lifelike and error-free as possible. Have the mental discipline to do this exercise obsessively until the sense of a perfect swing is internalized. The body and mind will remember each sensation and then work to reproduce them when you are next on an actual golf course.

Maltz was hardly the first person to offer this advice. In *The Power of Positive Thinking*, Norman Vincent Peale recommends: "Formulate and stamp indelibly on your mind a mental picture of yourself as succeeding. Hold this picture tenaciously. Never permit it to fade. Your mind will seek to develop the picture."

I do not play golf so I cannot guarantee that this exercise will improve anyone's game. But I do use visualization virtually every day in my own life. The technique helps me feel positive and prepared which always improves the odds of success. When scheduled to deliver a speech, I hole up in my basement several days in advance. I imagine standing on stage staring out at hundreds of audience members as they wait expectantly for me to begin. I mentally talk through each segment of my outline visualizing all of the major (and minor) points. I take my time and think about being bold and assured so that a confident attitude carries over into my demeanor. Nothing should be left to chance. In my mind, this mental practice always begins with one thought: "If the speech goes perfectly, this is exactly how it will proceed." I repeat individual steps in my brain as often as possible (frequently after I am lying in bed at night) until every aspect of the presentation is ready. Before stepping in front of the live audience, I want to be calm and poised—as if the speech had already taken place and was a huge success. At that point, I simply replicate the steps that have been so carefully visualized in my mind.

Soon after I started practicing mental imagery exercises in hopes of becoming more successful, I began to read about other practitioners. One of the most famous examples is described in the August 13, 1984, edition of *Time* magazine in a review of the summer Olympics.

"The night before the finals in women's gymnastics last week, Mary Lou Retton, 16, lay in bed at the Olympic Village, conjuring. It was an established ritual for her, no different from the imaginings of a hundred other nights. 'I see myself hitting all my routines, doing everything perfectly,' says Retton. 'I imagine all the moves and go through them with the image in my mind.' The following day, the spunky Retton led the U.S. team through a stylish and rousingly high-flying performance. . . . The moment fully lived up to Retton's expectations: 'It was just like I dreamed it, the excitement, the tension, the crowd, the feeling you have standing on the podium with an Olympic medal.' . . . Two nights later, everything that glittered was around Retton's neck. She won the gold medal in the all-around championship, the most coveted prize in gymnastics, since it marks the winner as the finest gymnast in the world."

Mental imagery is a fascinating concept, but how can it help your efforts to succeed? If a person is not participating in the Olympics or delivering a speech, what is the benefit? I find visualization works best when coupled with daily planning so that it becomes part of the normal routine of life. John Ruskin, an influential art critic in England during the 19th century, kept a stone on his desk with one word scratched into its surface:

Today

Although the sentiment appeals to me, I would have selected an even more immediate admonition:

Now

As we strive to reach Level-3 goals, success or failure boils down to making good use of time right now. *For me, the primary benefit of visualization is not in imagining the successful completion of the few large goals of life, but rather the smallest parts of each day.* "I successfully preformed this action in my mental preparation last night and now I will do it exactly the same way for real." Whether the task is massive or infinitesimally small, the only time that matters is the one in which we reside. How do we prepare in order to make the most of the current moment?

An earlier discussion recommended creating a time budget for each new 24 hours. If the upcoming day turns out to be absolutely perfect, what will be accomplished and when? Now, begin to take that planning process a step further. As a start, look at your list of activities for tomorrow and pick the most important one. Visualize that process just as Mary Lou Retton mentally practiced her upcoming gymnastic program. Think about what you want to have happen and then imagine each successive step falling perfectly into place. Retton was not doing anything that you cannot do. Absolutely not. Although a gold medal probably does not await your efforts, gaining success in the many individual tasks of life is an essential habit to develop.

> "If you take care of the small things,
> the big things take care of themselves.
> You can gain more control over your life by
> paying closer attention to the little things."
>
> Emily Dickinson

Visualization requires practice. Mental discipline is necessary or the mind will wander. Here are examples that might help get you started.

Example One: Assume tomorrow's schedule indicates the need to spend an hour writing a report on a recent action that occurred at your workplace. Although the task is rather mundane, it needs to be performed efficiently. Nothing is ever gained by doing a poor job. Find a quiet location and take a few moments to visualize the procedures necessary to create this document. Image the writing moving forward with wonderful alacrity. The words flow from your mind easily and clearly. Sentences and paragraphs come together in a logical, understandable progression. Written thoughts paint a true likeness of the event without confusion or contradiction. Feel the satisfaction as you gain a sense of accomplishment. We all experience moments in life when an activity just clicks and moves along with the precision of a well-oiled machine. That is the mental image you want. Feel the paper and pencil in your hands. Visualization should be as realistic as possible. Note the sensation of tapping on the keyboard. Picture your mind functioning with clarity and effectiveness. Mentally repeat this routine as often as possible.

Then, when the actual report is to be written, be confident and stay calm. Your mind and body know what needs to be done. Emulate the steps already envisioned. Follow the mental imagery and stack the odds of a successful project in your favor.

Example Two: Students in college often claim they study for hours each night with poor results. They become frustrated by their inefficiency and want to do better. Assume you are scheduled to study several hours tomorrow in preparation for a test. Excellent use of that time is imperative. A good grade is essential. Once again, mental imagery can help get you ready and improve the chances for a successful experience. The day before start with the feeling that those hours of study will pass exactly as desired. No time is wasted. Previously random ideas and rules essential to each topic begin to make sense. You see how they all fit together in a logical pattern. Your study time adds plenty of points to your knowledge. Visualize sitting at a desk, picking up a pencil and beginning to work practice questions while taking careful notes. Your mind is clear. You are mentally strong, not sleepy or bored. Important information jumps out of every sentence. Complexities start to make sense. You are not tempted to check Facebook. Neither Twitter nor text messages distracts your attention from the task at hand. You are so focused that noise and commotion are not a problem. Faith in your ability grows as you operate at a high level of efficiency and energy. Visualization helps train both mind and body to function in the desired manner. Create the mental picture of a perfect study session and then follow that image when the appointed time arrives.

Example Three: Over the years, hundreds of students have sat in my office fighting back tears, baffled by a poor test grade. They are certain of their knowledge and cannot fathom why they underperformed on the examination. They believe fervently that their understanding was far superior to the grade. Students talk about becoming nervous and flustered during a test or confess that they simply panicked. Visualization exercises performed a day or so in advance could have helped them avoid such pitfalls and maximize their grades.

When faced with an upcoming test, create a mental picture of walking into the classroom relaxed and confident. You have studied hard and learned the material. You are ready to display that knowledge and earn a good grade. Visualize reading the questions with a deep level of concentration. As you analyze each one, see yourself uncovering the various tricks hidden within the words and numbers. The questions make sense and the answers are apparent. Even when challenged by an unexpected twist, you remain calm. You are not nervous, nor distracted. Important concepts rush back into your brain. You move rapidly through the test because you are so well prepared. Repeat this mental imagery in advance of the test until it feels natural.

I refer to this as "confidence visualization." Consider every possible detail and imagine that the entire experience is perfect. How would that feel? That is the mental picture you want as you prepare for the important accomplishments of each new day whether it is a test, project, presentation, or any other challenge.

I recently watched a video about the Islamic art exhibited at the Metropolitan Museum of Art in New York City. One of the pieces was a wonderful earthenware bowl, approximately 1,000 years old. I still wonder how it has managed to survive over the centuries without being cracked or crushed. The most striking feature was the painted glaze on the outer rim which was drawn in a lovely, intricate pattern. The instructor explained that this striking design had been formed by using the words "planning before work protects you from regret; prosperity and peace" written in the Arabic language of the bowl's creator. The artist applied those words to the surface with such precise forethought that they exactly filled the space. And, the message has been passed down now for 1,000 years.

Planning (both mental visualization and physical practice) are essential for stacking the odds of success in your favor. Prosperity and peace can never be guaranteed, but scheduling out the work to be done and then using mental imagery to increase efficiency always helps improve the chances.

Closing Activity: I suppose the closing activity here is obvious. Consider all those tasks that you hope to accomplish tomorrow. For practice, pick one that should take approximately an hour. Write down in detail each step that must be performed for that particular job to be accomplished at an optimum level. What should happen first, then second, and so on? Then, visualize each of those individual tasks performed by you with such high quality that the desired result is perfect. Mentally walk through the entire process creating a clear image of what needs to occur. Spend time creating a lifelike feeling for each of the individual steps. Feel the pride that will come from a job well done.

The following day perform the work as envisioned. Allow your mind and body to complete the job just as remembered from the visualization exercise. Mental imagery should be a constant component of your planning that leads to an increase in success. Now, the time has come to discover that for yourself.

Ten: Look beyond the Superficial to See What Creates Success

Mark Rothko was a celebrated artist who worked during the middle part of the 20th century. The website for the National Gallery of Art in Washington, DC, provides this assessment of his influence on the world of art.

"One of the preeminent artists of his generation, Mark Rothko is closely identified with the New York School, a circle of painters that emerged during the 1940s as a new collective voice in American art. During a career that spanned five decades, he created a new and impassioned form of abstract painting."

In 2009, the play *Red* opened in London before eventually moving to Broadway in New York City and then throughout the United States. The action is set in Rothko's studio and consists of conversations between the artist and his young assistant. *Red* was recently staged here in Richmond, Virginia. I am no theatre expert, but found the play funny, interesting, and insightful. Although the entire production is a fascinating look at Rothko's ideas and personality, one short monologue about an Henri Matisse painting really caught my attention. Those few lines have reverberated through my brain numerous times since that evening.

In this particular scene, Rothko is describing the evolution of the unique style that made his art both famous and influential. At a critical point early in his development as an artist, he discovered a work that truly intrigued him: Matisse's *The Red Studio* at the Museum of Modern Art in New York City. Initially, he was baffled by how Matisse managed to create the painting's stunning effect. Unlike most people, Rothko could not let go of the need to understand what he was seeing. How did the artist produce such a powerful impact? What caused this mix of oils to be so mesmerizing? Returning to the museum each day, he stood in front of the painting for hours analyzing Matisse's techniques and talent. According to the play, the daily pilgrimage continued until Rothko was able to unravel the mystery to his satisfaction. He had a tenacious need to see more deeply—a characteristic that enabled him to grow artistically as he began to comprehend the secrets that made this painting great.

He did not buy a book about Matisse and fall in line with some expert's opinion.

He did not take a class on Matisse so that a teacher could describe various theories about the work.

He did not call Matisse on the telephone and ask for an explanation.

He did not go online and pull up Matisse's resume to discover the school where the artist had studied.

No. Rothko went back day after day, hour after hour, and stared obsessively at *The Red Studio* working to penetrate the wonder of its composition. He was witnessing a work of genius which inspired him so completely that he was unable to rest until he mentally captured that essence. Only then could those secrets be assimilated into his own artistic talent. *You cannot implement what you do not understand.*

Why did Rothko not just go to the studio and learn to paint by practicing more? The truth is that we are only human; everyone needs guidance. Virtually no one succeeds without external inspiration. The real question is whether you (yes, YOU) will settle for the superficial or, like Rothko, persistently push into the depths of success to gain the insight that will impact your life.

We all face such choices throughout life. In school, teachers urge students to dig into a great work of literature to appreciate its meaning and symbolism. But, they can always choose to settle for a brief perusal of Cliffs Notes. Many opt for the easier path. That route is not as demanding. Apparently, they are not convinced that in-depth analysis would provide sufficient reward. Rothko believed completely and refused to quit until every drop of guidance had been milked from Matisse's work.

Too often, rather than investing the effort to understand greatness, we charge off to find success with only a copy of Cliffs Notes in our hands.

Inspirational guidance comes from many sources, but always has two components. Mark Rothko became a renowned artist because he possessed both.

- Belief in the importance of the person, object, or task has to exist. Rothko's attention was completely ensnared by *The Red Studio*. He was certain it was a work of artistic brilliance.

- He achieved understanding. Many fail to dig deep enough to comprehend the undergirding on which that success is built. They are impressed by the result, but never determine exactly why. Rothko was not satisfied with the obvious. He looked closer and closer.

Try an experiment. While wandering through daily life, ask the people you encounter to identify their heroes. Whom do they admire? Whom would they most like to emulate? Most people, especially if ambitious, will probably respond with one or more names almost immediately. Steve Jobs might be mentioned, or Bill Gates, or perhaps a government leader, or a sports figure. Mother Teresa is a possible choice because of her incredible work with the poor. Having a hero helps us solidify our own personal identity. A few years back, Gatorade did a series of commercials based on the desire to "Be like Mike" – taking advantage of the public and its wish to share in the talent and success of Michael Jordan.

But, the follow-up question is more insightful: What makes this person so special? For many, answers quickly turn vague. The hero has energy. The hero has determination. The hero has enthusiasm or the ability to work hard. The hero has ideas. What does that tell us? Millions of people have those characteristics. Such responses show belief in the person without deep understanding. No true guidance has been gained. Actions and results have not been analyzed closely enough to identify reasons for admiration. Rothko did not care about Matisse or his personality. Rothko did not ask whether the artist worked 3 hours each day or 22, whether he was cheerful or dour. Such traits were not relevant to Rothko's Level-3 goals. Standing in front of that one painting, he focused entirely on the visual impact. How did Matisse create this masterpiece? The search for an answer continued each day until Rothko believed he understood the secrets. Only then could he begin to develop his own greatness.

How often do you study success with that intensity? For Level-3 goals, analysis is an important step in stacking the odds of success in your favor. When face to face with greatness, are you a bit obsessed by the desire to uncover the key actions that led to this level of success? Can you see past the superficial to the truly essential?

Bobby Knight is a legendary (and controversial) retired college basketball coach. Many years ago, he was interviewed on a television program. Nothing about the show has stayed in my memory other than one specific question and his response. The reporter asked Coach Knight to identify the single most important attribute of a great basketball player. As I watched, a lot of answers passed rapidly through my mind such as the ability to shoot well, or jump high, or run fast. I also considered the need for good eye-hand coordination, or the sheer determination necessary to practice for hours on end or, perhaps, the stamina to play with maximum energy for an entire game. An intense desire to win is another reasonable guess.

I was incorrect on all counts. Much to my surprise at the time, Coach Knight did not settle on any of those choices. According to him, the most important skill in basketball is the ability to play the game at full speed while still seeing what is happening. An individual who sees the action clearly as it unfolds is most likely to make the appropriate play. In hindsight, he was right and I was wrong. A truly great player can see what each of the other nine people on the court is doing before taking any action. Talent alone is never enough. During games, many superb athletes seem to become lost and make poor decisions. Announcers often comment that a particular player is "just not in the flow of the game tonight." A few, though, always appear to be in control of the entire court, like a dance master directing a ballet troupe. *They have the knack for seeing the action as a logical pattern.* That "knack" probably required thousands of hours of practice. But, those players are the ones who usually orchestrate a win. Larry Bird, one of the most savvy basketball players of all time, once said: "I always know what's happening on the court. I see a situation occur, and I respond."

Connections are rarely made between modern art and basketball. However, an essential ingredient for success can be identified from Mark Rothko's actions and Bobby Knight's words. For greatness to be useful, you must learn to see clearly. Success is rarely possible if you are operating blindly.

Practice. Start today. Look for the success that surrounds you and attempt to see it more clearly. Try to understand how it was accomplished. That is a worthwhile endeavor. Identify patterns that lead to success. By determining what happened and why, you can meld the guidance into your own actions. Be like Mark Rothko. Spot success and then work to uncover its secrets.

Some people develop the ability to see because of inspiration, others out of necessity. Here are two examples.

Example One: On a college campus, many people talk about becoming excellent teachers. That goal is commonly espoused. However, teaching is rarely easy. Various strategies and techniques abound. Students in every class have their own particular set of issues. Some learn best at a particular speed and others in a specific way. Frequently, the personal issues that most people face threaten to intrude into classroom performance. Regardless of the tumult in their lives, students still need to be prepared for class, engaged in the discussions, and able to reason through complicated theories and practical problems. Teaching is a wonderfully rewarding occupation, but success is a challenge. Teaching 30 students often seems the equivalent of juggling 30 flaming batons.

I won a teaching award several years ago. As a result, college professors occasionally sit in on my class to view what transpires. Those 50 minutes are helter-skelter and often resemble the inside of a pinball machine. Much to my surprise, visitors rarely raise questions. After the session, most thank me for an interesting experience and drift away.

For whatever reason, they do not appear inclined to peek below the surface to better explore what they have seen. Have I provided any guidance? Possibly, but I am never sure if either belief or understanding has been enhanced by passive observation.

Last year, a local journalist asked to attend class because she hoped to become a teacher. From the opening bell, she took copious notes. She appeared to be documenting every action that took place. At the end of class, she followed me to my office and began posing well-conceived questions. We talked for nearly an hour as she sought to grasp the minute details of the process she had witnessed. Like Mark Rothko, she was working to pull clarity out of what seemed superficially to be chaos. Her interest did not mean she was trying to teach like me. That was not the point. She wanted to understand the intricate details of the educational experience so she could develop her own style. Many questions started with "Exactly what were you doing in this situation?" or "How would you react to this type of occurrence?" She sought guidance. The desire to learn pushed her to figure out what she had seen. She did not ask for short cuts. She wanted to understand.

Example Two: A few years back, a student in one of my classes seemed intelligent, but never walked into class prepared. Consequently, she always trailed behind in the conversation trying desperately to comprehend what we were discussing. On the first test of the semester, she made a D. After that, I watched closely for any sign of improvement. Unfortunately, she continued to arrive unprepared. On the second test, she made another D. Soon, she was sitting in my office nearly hysterical because she had never before made such low grades. She claimed (probably truthfully) that she had done well throughout her years in school by taking careful notes which she then memorized and handed back to the teacher on subsequent tests. My exams required critical thinking and she had underestimated the need to adapt.

This student's semester was on the verge of catastrophe unless she could muster an immediate turnaround. My advice went something like this: "I have told the class all semester that everyone must be prepared walking into the room each day in order to understand what is happening. You have chosen to ignore those warnings. We move fast and without that readiness you cannot follow the discussion. Memorizing your notes is a waste of time. The material is complex and very important. I want you to understand it."

I then made a suggestion: "Success in this class requires preparation. At our next class, make it your personal goal to be the best prepared student in the room. Just for this one day, try that tactic. Work as many hours as it takes so that you enter the room knowing more than anyone else. I think class coverage will start to make much more sense." She agreed to try. Being a bit cynical, I immediately thought to myself: "She is going to be the best prepared student in that class when pigs learn to fly."

Well, I am delighted to confess that I was wrong. At the next session, I asked her the very first question and made sure it was quite difficult. Without hesitation, she provided an excellent answer, one that required serious study. I asked another question and got an even better answer. From that day forward, she was the best student in class. She arrived prepared each day and participated actively in class discussion. She made an A on the third test and an A on the final exam and a B+ for the semester.

What happened? That is simple. Out of sheer desperation, she opened her eyes to see that preparation was, indeed, necessary. By finally learning how success was obtained, she turned what looked like absolute failure into a good grade. At that point, she had both belief and understanding of the role she had to play in this class to achieve success.

"The things you think are the disasters in your life are not the disasters really. Almost anything can be turned around: out of every ditch, a path, if you can only see it."

Hilary Mantel, *Bring Up the Bodies*

Closing Activity: We will probably have difficulty gaining guidance directly from our heroes. Unfortunately, Steve Jobs and Mother Teresa are dead and Bill Gates is not likely to return phone calls or even text messages. The composition of greatness must be uncovered and only with some effort. Make the search part of your daily journey. Start by becoming better aware of the success that you encounter in the routine moments of life.

Buy a note pad or use your smartphone and begin to keep a "success diary." While moving through life each day, take note of those people, objects, events, and the like that you judge to be successful. Open your eyes and see the success that is all around you.

--A waitress who makes you smile with her pleasant efficiency is a success.

--A television program that is exceptionally well written is a success.

--A parent whose young children are happy and obedient is a success.

--A minister who provides hope to a congregation is a success.

--An ice skater who executes a graceful jump is a success.

--A song on the radio that pulls at your emotions is a success.

Enjoy the process of looking. *Learning to be successful should be fun.* Always be on the watch. The most impressive success stories can also be the best hidden. Try to add 5-10 listings to this diary every day. The exercise alone will make you a better person. We live in a bitter and cynical time. If you become oblivious to the success around you, inspirational guidance will never appear.

Eventually, choose one individual from your list (friend, relative, acquaintance at work, or the like). You have glimpsed success in some aspect of that person's life. Ask to meet, possibly for coffee or ice cream, because you want to talk about the success you have observed. Most people will be greatly flattered that you have noticed them.

"You seem successful at doing this particular task. I have watched and you do it so very well and seem to enjoy the process. I want that feeling for myself. How have you made that success happen?"

Never be satisfied with superficial or modest answers. "I worked hard" or "I was lucky" might both be true, but do not provide useful information. Be like Mark Rothko. Talk with the person and ask questions until you understand the genesis of that success. Avoid superficial distractions. Success requires inspirational guidance and that only comes from both belief and understanding.

Eleven: Deeper Understanding Grows With a Second Look

I have described and analyzed success in these pages from many different perspectives. Now is probably a good time to pause and reflect for a moment. Simply racing from one page to the next reduces (or eliminates) the possibility of significant benefit. The goal is not to finish reading the entire book in record time, but rather to consider how each section can best provide practical assistance.

- Which of these ideas is most likely to help you (yes, YOU) stack the odds of success in your favor?
- Which suggestions seem particularly relevant to your life and aspirations?

Avoid being a passive reader. Focus on those thoughts with the most potential to be beneficial. Assessment provides guidance by pointing out where to exert a higher level of attention.

Periodic review helps solidify understanding—a concept that was hammered home to me during my senior year in high school. In those days, athletes received "letters" for their efforts. These symbols were sewn onto jackets to be worn proudly through the halls. To a 17 year old, the outfit looked wonderfully impressive. A deep desire crept over me for the coolness of a letter jacket. Unfortunately, at 5' 8," 125 pounds, and with no apparent athletic ability, I was unlikely to ever be awarded a letter for participation in football, basketball, track, or any other sport.

Never one to be discouraged by minor adversity, I recruited three friends to form a debate team—our version of an athletic endeavor. Because no team had existed for years, we automatically gained official recognition. And, as we well knew, a school letter could be earned for debate. Out of extreme kindness, our elderly algebra teacher agreed to serve as coach. (In my memory, she still appears elderly although she was probably younger than I am today.) She had participated in debate and provided considerable assistance to four such rank amateurs. One piece of advice from that experience has resonated with me and affected my work since those glory days. Throughout the debate season, she told us time and again:

> If you want people to remember what you say
> tell them what you are going to say
> then tell them what you have to say
> and finally tell them what you just said.

Excellent advice! If a person hears an idea or concept only one time (no matter how important), the information is rarely assimilated fast enough to make a permanent mark on the memory. To use a more common expression, it does not sink in. The childhood game of Telephone invariably demonstrates the problem. The last player in line hears words completely unrelated to the message originally whispered to the first. Although each listener might be quite attentive, successful conveyance of information requires repetition and review. First let the audience know what you are going to say, then say it, and conclude by reminding them of what you said. Never underestimate the importance of programmed redundancy.

In football, basketball, and most other team sports, the coach can stop play by calling timeout. Players tend to lose their concentration during a game because of exhaustion and excitement. Results begin to suffer. A timeout provides opportunity for renewal. For those few minutes, the coach attempts to recharge the team's energy level (probably in a loud and stern voice): "Don't get away from our game plan. Remember how you are supposed to run these plays. Don't lose your focus. Go out there and do the work that we have discussed." During that pause in the action, players are reminded once again of what has already been said.

The same need for a break occurs in daily life. Dashing about every moment of the day frequently becomes counterproductive. In the helter-skelter world of the 21st century, our sense of direction and purpose often takes flight. The focus on dreams and success begins to fade. A brief respite for reflection provides a chance to renew our enthusiasm and pull us away from failure. Retrospective examination also brings earlier thoughts back into our consciousness for additional consideration.

For that reason, I am calling a quick timeout. As my high school debate coach might have advised, I want to introduce a bit of redundancy into these writings by asking you to pause and reconsider the ideas described so far. Look back with heightened awareness. Deeper understanding grows with a second look. You can now bundle together pieces of different stories to provide an overall strategy, a "thought provoking tapestry about success" (as I described this collection of essays in an early chapter). Try to connect seemingly unrelated ideas to form a consistent philosophy if you are serious about becoming more successful. You will not achieve an increased level of accomplishment by the performance of random acts but rather through creation of a total life environment—a complete mindset—designed to stack the odds of success in your favor.

Closing Activity: As a basis for review, I will insert the closing activity here rather than at the end of this essay. In the book's first few pages, I recommended evaluation as a skill worth developing. We all face limitations imposed by the constraints of daily existence. In other words, we must make choices. No matter how hard we try, people cannot take advantage of every opportunity. Alternatives must be analyzed. We must study each one to weigh and judge their importance. What future action is most beneficial? Which strategy should we adopt?

Therefore, during this timeout, reexamine the previous pages and consider the various suggestions. As a structure for your evaluation, identify the five statements that seem most helpful in your personal quest for success. I have offered a wide array of ideas in these pages. Which can actually be most beneficial? Make judgments; be decisive.

Below is my top list. After rereading all of the previous material, I identified nine possibilities that I have narrowed down to these final five. Do not read my choices until after determining your own. Avoid being influenced by my thinking. Positive action is more likely to result when working with selections that you found especially meaningful on a personal level.

<u>COUNTDOWN OF MY TOP FIVE LIST FROM THE PREVIOUS CHAPTERS</u>

NUMBER FIVE

The writings in this volume form a trap, one that is intended to lure you into doing your own thinking because that is the only avenue to real accomplishments.

With concerted effort, success can become a more common occurrence, but nothing is guaranteed. To improve the odds, be willing to think deeply about each Level-3 goal, not just now and then, but on a daily basis. That is one reason success is so elusive for many people. You have to pay the price. No one can think for you. And, those thoughts cannot simply be "I want it!" but rather "How does it happen?" and "What do I need to do next?" and "Which sacrifices are required?" Study the greatness around you. You accomplish nothing by dwelling on the superficial. Analyze success methodically and absorb the lessons that are uncovered. The thinking is entirely up to you.

As is likely obvious from these writings, I am fascinated by quotations that provide guidance and insight, words that are inspirational and make me think. Nevertheless, only two quotes are taped to the wall over my desk here at home. One comes from the Zen master Linji. It is the often repeated saying (referred to as a kōan): "If you meet the Buddha, kill the Buddha."

I am not a Zen scholar, but imagine that many explanations for these strange words (that have been passed down for over 1,000 years) must exist. Perhaps, the ultimate meaning is intended to be different for each person. I like that thought. For me, this riddle teaches that the answers to life's challenges must ultimately come from inside each of us. Outside suggestions and advice provide assistance but, for the important questions of life, no one can arrive at the answers for you except you. In the search for success, if external solutions (the Buddha) are encountered, they must be false. Do not be deceived. You will find no answers as you make your way along the path. You must discover them within yourself. They are only available through the fruits of your own thinking.

Success cannot be bought or begged. The Zen quote is taped to the wall in this office as a daily reminder that my success is my responsibility.

NUMBER FOUR

Try to be better than yourself.

This wonderful quote from William Faulkner applies to success in all its various forms. To succeed, a person must stretch beyond past accomplishments, beyond even what one believes to be possible. Often we are excessively modest and self-deprecating. That tendency can be counterproductive because it reduces expectations. Never provide an excuse for failure. In truth, we are blessed with enormous talent. Every person has capabilities that greatly exceed what can ever be imagined. Each of us possesses the ability to make a genuine difference in this world. The key is to tap into that enormous reserve—an action that only comes when we are forced to abandon our personal comfort zones. Avoid settling for short cuts and easy answers. We all have unlimited possibilities, but they are only available to those who are willing to push through self-imposed boundaries.

On the road to success, many get stuck in ruts and never escape. That is a common human malady. Time passes and we make no discernable progress. We waste our potential. I have always admired individuals who are continuously inventive over long periods of time. They succeed and then try something different and succeed again. That impresses me. Bob Dylan recorded "Blowing in the Wind" in 1962 and that song alone ensured his fame. In 1965, he released "Like a Rolling Stone," one of the greatest works in the history of rock and roll. "Lay Lady Lay" is a classic country piece from 1969. The mysterious "Tangled Up in Blue" followed in 1975. A favorite album—*Love and Theft*—appeared in 2001, and I view the song "Tin Angel" (2012) as one of his more interesting works. That is 50 years of productive, innovative success. And, he continues to write and perform. Bob Dylan is a person who appears to have succeeded in trying to be better than himself.

Likewise, Pablo Picasso is one of the most popular artists in history. He created masterpiece after masterpiece from his early teens until he was over 90. One of the most incredible aspects of this proliferation was that his art was constantly changing—often in dramatic ways. Whether young or old, his work rarely became predictable. Picasso pushed himself to evolve and be different and, therefore, better. He is famous for his blue period, rose period, African-influenced period, analytical cubism, synthetic cubism, neoclassical style, surrealism, and many more. He seemed to be obsessively driven to stretch the limits of what could be accomplished.

Such people inspire success. Both Dylan and Picasso became famous early in life, but never stopped working to develop the reach of their talents. When setting Level-3 goals, make sure they challenge you to try to be better than yourself.

NUMBER THREE

Success, to a great extent, is born of a story we tell ourselves.

Any discussion of success must eventually return to two words: attitude and confidence. Without them, extraordinary achievements become virtually impossible. Nevertheless, simply acknowledging their significance accomplishes nothing. Saying that a person needs an upbeat attitude that creates confidence will not make it so. Attitude and confidence must be woven into the fabric of everyday experience. They need to become an integral part of the story that we tell ourselves to explain the essence of who we are.

When I was growing up in the 1950s, Walt Disney was a man on television every Sunday evening who introduced a program bearing his name. On that ancient television set, he appeared to be a genuine and kind person who was delighted to welcome the audience into his office to watch a great new show. His enthusiasm was contagious.

Obviously, the company that Disney founded decades ago has grown into a gigantic conglomerate with operations around the world. Revenues in 2012 exceeded $42 billion which is roughly $6 for every man, woman, and child on the entire planet. I consider myself a student of success and The Walt Disney Company certainly qualifies for that title. What basic principles have provided the inspiration for each new generation of workers who continue to create a thriving, innovative environment? What foundation can a person establish that generates ever increasing prosperity over an extended period of time? That is the type of question about success that I like to ponder.

Last year, I visited Walt Disney World in Orlando with my grandchildren. One afternoon, we were strolling through the Magic Kingdom near a construction site where I discovered a number of quotations from Mr. Disney that had been affixed to a temporary fence. One caught my attention and immediately helped me understand the philosophy that has enabled this organization to achieve incredible success for so many years.

"When we consider a project, we really study it—not just the surface idea, but everything about it. And when we go into that new project, we believe in it all the way. We have confidence in our ability to do it right. And we work hard to do the best possible job."

In just four sentences, this story lays out the attitude and confidence on which Disney's success was built. It provides a perfect roadmap for the company's many accomplishments from theme parks to movies. As stated often in these pages, success does not happen by accident. No better example of that rule can be found than this one. Early in his career, Mr. Disney identified the necessary ingredients for success and the leaders have continued to preach that message to guide employees and assure customers.

Break this quotation into its pieces and what story do you see?

(1) Study is necessary and the company will not be satisfied with a superficial effort.

(2) Belief runs throughout the organization in its ability to make appropriate decisions.

(3) Confidence exists that each action will be performed in the best way.

(4) Employees are capable of the hard work that is required for success.

NUMBER TWO

Improvement is necessary for success and most improvement comes as a direct result of a person's reaction to failure.

Any company or person who repeats (and then lives) such a story should encounter few limitations in its quest to succeed.

Failure for most people is devastating. The impulse to give up and quit is often the overwhelming initial reaction. Everyone harbors self-doubts and failure brings them out like a pack of howling dogs. The knowledge that success can never be guaranteed will hang like a dark shroud over even the most exciting adventure. The mere fear of rejection is enough to snuff out the dreams of many Level-3 goals. Often, the response to failure is the critical juncture in a person's march toward success. The decision can come down to a stark choice: surrender now or have the faith to keep moving forward.

The books of Dr. Seuss (Theodor Geisel) have had a positive influence on probably more children than those of almost any other author in history. From *The Cat in the Hat* and *Green Eggs and Ham* to the final book published before his death—*Oh, the Places You'll Go!*—Dr. Seuss engaged and delighted millions of young (and old) readers. The world would be a far darker place without those witty and inventive works.

However, when Geisel began his career in the 1930s, the first book he wrote and illustrated was judged a worthless failure by many experts.

And to Think That I Saw It on Mulberry Street presented a very different type of book for the children of that time. Almost no one recognized its unique genius. Consequently, publishers rejected the work 27 times before it was finally accepted by Vanguard Press. Imagine going to the mailbox day after day and receiving so many rejection letters. Over two dozen editors informed Geisel that his work was not good enough. That had to be terribly discouraging. Anyone else would likely have concluded that those publishing professionals knew their business and the book really was unworthy. If Geisel had given up after the 27th rejection, children might never have experienced the pleasure of reading Dr. Seuss. Luckily for us all, he believed in his creative talent. He refused to abandon his dream. The rest is history.

In any study of successful individuals, Theodor Geisel's story is not unique. Much the same happened to Pablo Picasso. During a recent visit to Barcelona, I toured the Picasso Museum where a guide recounted an early setback in the artist's career. When just 19, Picasso held his first public exhibition. Imagine his excitement. A total of 150 paintings were displayed in a local café. Not one sold. None. Customers came and went each day, but were unimpressed and chose not to acquire an early Picasso. Apparently, no one expected serious talent from this young artist and, therefore, failed to see it hanging on the wall in plain sight.

Picasso could have been devastated. In a similar situation, many people would have tossed their paint brushes in the trash and started looking for a job. Instead, throughout life, his reaction to adversity was to work harder. In fact, one of Picasso's most famous sayings alludes to this response: "les autres parlent moi je travaille" (others talk, I work). As a result of that tenacity, he became a legendary figure admired by millions. Perhaps he altered his style or adjusted his technique. But he did not quit. He refused to let rejection put a halt to his quest for greatness.

No one succeeds every day, not even superstars like Dr. Seuss and Pablo Picasso. After establishing Level-3 goals, be ready to face all types of hindrances. That is what the road to success looks like—a rough path cluttered with obstacles. It might even appear to have a solid wall standing in the way. Rather than quitting, step back and evaluate the situation. Then, as Michael Jordan advised early in this book, "Don't turn around and give up. Figure out how to climb it, go through it, or work around it."

NUMBER ONE

Most successful people have a few Level-3 goals that light up their days and nights and push them forward, often at blinding speed.

First and foremost, this book is about setting Level-3 goals that will entice you to work as hard as possible to accomplish them. Without the inspiration that comes from such challenges, we limit our success to the mundane, everyday affairs of life. Deprived of the guidance they provide, we lose the direction and desire necessary for success. If life today seems dull or out of focus, look to fix your Level-3 goals.

To many sports fans, Vince Lombardi is the greatest football coach of all time. He created a dynasty with the Green Bay Packers, a team that rarely lost while he was coach. However, in his second season (1960), the Packers played for the pro football championship, but lost when the last play was stopped a few yards short of the winning touchdown. Coach Lombardi was outraged that his team had come so close to victory and been turned back. In the locker room after the game, he informed the players in no uncertain terms: "This will never happen again. You will never lose another championship."

And, he backed up that promise. It never happened again as long as Vince Lombardi was coach. The Packers won championships in 1961, 1962, 1965, 1966, and 1967. The team did not win all their games after 1960, but they won virtually every game of importance. After this early defeat, he redoubled his efforts and drove the players to bring them up to championship caliber. The man knew what he wanted and went out and made it happen. Life should always work that way.

Coach Lombardi never heard the term "Level-3 goal," but, for him, winning championships met the definition. First, the objective was a challenge, not easy to reach. "The hard is what makes it great" as Tom Hanks' character says in *A League of Their Own*. Second, Coach Lombardi clearly had a burning desire to win championships. It was not an idle fantasy. He was willing to do the work to make it happen. Without that degree of ambition, a person's potential for success is always limited. If you study true success in sports, business, school, art, or any other venue, a Level-3 goal will be involved.

I am a firm believer that the world would be a better place if more people took the time to identify their Level-3 goals. Coach Lombardi was a winner because he had a Level-3 goal that provided a focal point for the football part of his life. He knew the success he wanted. In this book, the most important question is always going to be: What challenging success do you really want to achieve?

Answer that question and you will be ready to get started on the path to success.

Okay, these are my five selections, the statements that have been the most meaningful for me to this point.

What about you? Your list is for you and can be completely different from mine. What ideas or suggestions have meant the most to you so far and why? Making such judgments is an important step in stacking the odds of success in your favor.

Twelve: Who Are You Really?

While driving several hours last week to visit my younger son and his family, I became bored by the monotony of the interstate highway system. I clicked on the radio for entertainment and was greeted with the rock and roll classic "Who Are You" by the Who from the late 70s. As with many events in life, the continual refrain "who are you?" started me thinking about attaining my Level-3 goals. When attempting to turn a serious dream into reality, having a meaningful answer for the question "who are you?" can make the difference between success and failure. Therefore, every person working to reach a Level-3 goal should consider adopting a personality model to guide the decision-making that is necessary along the way.

What do I mean by a "personality model?" I coined the term to signify a guidance technique that can help in moving work forward in a consistent fashion.

Throughout the preceding pages, I have stressed scheduling and visualization as preparatory steps in seeking success. This planning process is essential in structuring the work needed to reach Level-3 goals. In addition, a wide range of unexpected questions is almost inevitable. What should I do here? What action is needed there? How can I best respond to this problem? Months and even years can be invested in detailed planning but, beginning with the actual starting day, dozens of questions are likely to arise requiring practical decisions that were never even considered in advance. *Success often hinges on the ability to adapt formal plans into real time decisions in a matter of moments.*

To help prepare for practical questions that can alternate from the expected to the bizarre, start by identifying successful people you admire. Then, consider how they made decisions. The steps taken by General George S. Patton were different from those of the nurse Florence Nightingale. Pope John Paul II probably approached decision-making in an entirely different manner than Abraham Lincoln. When faced with important choices, a bank president and a heart surgeon almost certainly have their own unique ways of arriving at final conclusions. What methodology seems most akin to your thinking? No method is ever perfect. Settle on an approach that works best for you.

As a college student, I was frustrated by teachers who appeared to pull out different personalities for every class. One day they were kind and considerate, every student's best friend. At the next class, that first person had been replaced by a stern tyrant carved out of the Darth Vader mold. I referred to such professors as Dr. Jekyll and Mr. Hyde because their responses changed at each class for reasons that were never understood by the students. Decisions varied based on the persona of the day. I never minded either demanding teachers or kindly ones. But, I wanted them to make up their minds as to who they were so that I could react accordingly.

When I became a college teacher, I vowed to avoid this type of confusion. Almost from day one, I decided to adopt a personality model that could help me maintain consistency especially in my decision-making. Vince Lombardi was described in the previous chapter. He was my selection. From all that I read and heard at the time, his approach to leadership appealed to me. Looking back, much of what I have become as a teacher reflects my understanding of that philosophy. His legend showed me how to be what I wanted to be.

- He was famous for taking mediocre players and turning them into champions. That idea appealed to me in 1971. It appeals to me today. From my first day in front of a class, I have always sought to push every average student to achieve greatness. Anyone can teach brilliant students. I wanted to be involved in a more transformational process which is probably the reason I wrote this book.

- He understood his goal (to win championships) and did not allow himself to be distracted by tangential tasks. For genuine Level-3 goals, whether in sports, teaching, or other areas of life, seriously-focused attention is required. Too many people become bogged down in the minor details of life and lose sight of their primary objective. They fail without ever getting to the point of trying.

88

- He avoided making the process too complicated. We often overthink our jobs and get tied up in fancy solutions. Coach Lombardi was well-known for simplicity: "Some people try to find things in this game that don't exist but football is only two things—blocking and tackling." The work needed to achieve most goals in life can be boiled down to such basic tasks. Teaching, for example, is only two things—explaining and motivating.

- He approached work with a consistent philosophy that seemed to permeate his whole life. Throughout these pages, I have argued that success is most likely if based on an overall approach to life. The words of Coach Lombardi show a purpose that goes beyond football games. "Winning is not a sometime thing; it's an all the time thing. You don't win once in a while; you don't do things right once in a while; you do them right all the time. Winning is a habit."

Push people to achieve greatness, focus almost obsessively on the ultimate goal, keep every task as simple as possible, and develop a personal philosophy that will increase chances for success. Those standards still make perfect sense to me even after four decades.

In my first years as a teacher, I faced many complex problems and often found myself standing in front of a mirror searching for an answer to the question: "How would Vince Lombardi respond in this situation?" As a young person at the start of a career, that contemplation was an extremely helpful exercise. Regardless of the issue, I could envision his common sense solution which then guided my actions. In truth, the same internal conversation continues to assist me today. Pondering his likely answers has enabled me to be consistent in my work (I hope) and avoid becoming both Dr. Jekyll and Mr. Hyde to my students.

Unfortunately, Coach Lombardi died more than 40 years ago. If I were to pick a personality model today, who would it be? Do people like Vince Lombardi even exist today?

My 20 year old daughter follows a television show with the ironic title of *The Biggest Loser*. As I wander through the house, I occasionally sit down and watch an episode with her. A number of dramatically overweight individuals appear on the program and compete for several months to shed those excess pounds. Although numerous exercise and diet regiments are readily available, nothing has worked for these contestants. Most have failed many times over the years in various attempts to slim down. After years of futility, they have lost faith in themselves and their ability to become healthier. On the show, a trainer works with each person and the results are frequently amazing. Many lose more than 100 pounds by the end of the season.

I have now seen this show enough times to know that one of the trainers is Jillian Michaels. She has become famous because of her intense drive to help contestants in their fight to achieve a normal weight and healthy lifestyle. She believes people have the ability to gain control of their lives and sets out to teach them how to succeed. In a 2009 *Time* magazine article, she is quoted as saying: "People tend to think that metabolism is genetically predetermined. That you're either cursed or you're blessed. And that's not true. You can dramatically affect the expression of your metabolism and your biochemistry by the way you eat and the way you live."

If I were going to pick a personality model for my work today, Michaels would be an excellent choice. When watching the program, I am often struck that she is the Vince Lombardi of our time.

- She knows exactly what she wants to accomplish and pushes herself and others obsessively to achieve those results.
- She demands 100 percent effort from each member of her team. She is never easy on them. She accepts nothing less than their best.
- She views her job as tremendously important. By helping these individuals lose weight, she is literally trying to save lives. She believes that she can make a genuine difference. Without that attitude, no one would work so hard.
- She takes people who have faced a life of failure and helps them see themselves as winners.

- She appears to care for the contestants on the show. She treats them as human beings who deserve help.

As a personality model, how could she be better? Many people might not place her name at the top of their list of candidates for this position, but I can imagine looking into a mirror at work and asking myself: "I am facing a complicated problem that must be resolved. A decision is required right now. How would Jillian Michaels respond in this situation?" With a little thinking on my part, a reasonable solution is likely to become apparent.

But, that is guidance for me and my efforts. What personality model appeals to you? Consider every possibility. Let your brain run wild. Perhaps you prefer Steve Jobs (is tremendously inventive and enthusiastic but possibly a bit eccentric) or maybe Santa Claus (makes judgments as to which people have been naughty or nice with big rewards for the winners). *As Level-3 plans progress into the daily work of implementation, who are you really?* This choice requires you (yes, YOU) to think about the person you want to be when decisions must be made to turn plans for success into action.

Personality models are not necessarily easy to find. We live in cynical times. With modern technology, society knows as much about the bad traits people possess as the good. Athletes, politicians, entertainers, and other public figures seem to have a dark side that is more evident today than in the past as a result of omnipresent social media coverage. When talking with groups about seeking guidance for their actions, I often suggest that they create a "composite personality model." Select admirable characteristics from a variety of individuals. Instead of searching for a single perfect person, construct a whole list of attributes to help structure the decision-making process.

Study as many people as possible to uncover characteristics that stand out. I do this frequently. It is a good exercise for a person fascinated by success and greatness. Try to pinpoint the reasons a person is special. Baseball players often work well for this investigation. The game has a slow pace which provides more time for analysis than either basketball or soccer. The identity of each player is not hidden behind the bulky uniforms that disguise football and hockey players.

As an illustration, here are four baseball players with specific attributes that I admire. An outstanding composite personality model could be constructed from these individuals.

- *Mariano Rivera.* Rivera is generally viewed as the greatest "closer" in baseball history. A closer is the pitcher who enters the game near the end to save the victory when the outcome is in doubt. Virtually every time a closer plays, the situation is tense and he must perform at the highest possible level from the first pitch. Any little mistake can lead to an immediate loss. I cannot even estimate how often I have walked into a classroom thinking of myself as a closer who must be in top form from the first word if the students are going to achieve the progress they should. I love the response I feel to that self-induced pressure.

- *Lou Gehrig.* A few years back, baseball experts named Gehrig the greatest first baseman to ever play the game. In 1999, he received the most fan votes in the selection of the "All-Century Team." Those are impressive achievements but the level of skill is not the reason I view him as part of my personality model. Until 1925, Gehrig was a part-time player with limited success. On June 1 of that year, he substituted for another player and went on to play in 2,130 straight games—a record that was not broken for 60 years. Gehrig maintained a consistency of greatness, day after day, that is almost beyond belief. Even while injured or ill, he played and did his best. Many people are good at work one day but bad the next. Our efforts often mimic the up and down design of a roller coaster. Anyone who operates at a very high level every day for so many years is truly impressive. I try to bring that consistent excellence to my teaching.

- **Roy Hobbs.** Hobbs is not a real person but rather the main character in the book *The Natural* by Bernard Malamud. As a young man, he wants to become a professional baseball player and, early in the book, describes this overriding desire: "Sometimes when I walk down the street I bet people will say there goes Roy Hobbs, the best there ever was in the game." Okay, if you have read the book (the movie has an entirely different ending), things do not work out so well for Hobbs. Nevertheless, I love the level of ambition. Too often, we all want to be good, but few really burn to be great. As said previously in these pages, the world needs more people with a deep level of ambition. People would be happier and the world would function better with more Level-3 goals and less Level-1 fantasies. I have never walked into a classroom when I did not want to be the best teacher in the world. That is not a fantasy.

- **Brad Ausmus.** Occasionally, when driving home from campus, I listen to the show *Fresh Air* on NPR (National Public Radio). Terry Gross (or an associate) interviews a wide variety of interesting people. The discussions are often fabulous. One day a few years ago, the guest was Brad Ausmus, a retired catcher. He had played baseball in the major leagues for 18 years and is currently 7th on the all-time list for number of games caught. Every baseball fan knows that on occasion (especially when the game is going badly) the catcher runs out to the mound for a quick talk with the pitcher. Like every other baseball fan, I have always wondered what the catcher can possibly say. The person doing the radio interview asked that specific question of Ausmus. I loved the reply.

"My general rule was when I left the pitcher's mound after talking to any given pitcher, I want them to feel like they can get out of this situation. You know, baseball's a tough game. It's not as physically demanding as say football or hockey. But it's a tough game in the sense that it's pitch after pitch after pitch for 150 pitches a game for six straight months with very few days of rest. So when I left that mound, I wanted that pitcher, even if he was in the worst situation possible, if he was in bases loaded, no outs, with the tying run at third base in the bottom of the ninth inning—when I left that pitcher's mound, I wanted that pitcher to feel like 'hey, I've got a chance to get out of this.' So, my general rule was to be positive."

"My general rule was to be positive." I could not agree more. That is a rule we could all use.

A wonderful composite personality model can be constructed from these four individuals: function at your best from the first moment regardless of the pressure; be consistently excellent day-after-day for as long as possible; have a deep-held desire to be the best; and remain positive. Although no single individual exists like Vince Lombardi or Jillian Michaels, the guidance here still points directly toward success.

Closing Activity. Choosing a personality model requires a real understanding of who you are. For example, I am more like General Patton and less like Florence Nightingale. His decision-making style will probably appeal to me more than hers does.

A few years ago, one of the morning television programs (*Good Morning America*) set up an event where viewers were challenged to express themselves using just three words. What an interesting and clever idea! The only way to make that happen is to boil down inner thoughts to very essential elements. We are all complex individuals: What aspects of your being deserve to be highlighted? That is a question worth considering.

In that vein, I want to make a similar assignment here but in separate parts.

--Express the essence of what it means to be you in three words. Focus on who you really are. Avoid being trivial or funny. Take plenty of time. When satisfied, write these words in large letters on a sheet of paper that is then posted in a visible location that will be seen by you every day.

--Again using only three words, express the essence of what you want to be in exactly one year. How would you like to describe yourself one year from today? Write those three words on a different sheet and post them beside your first effort.

--Whenever you see these two lists side-by-side, challenge yourself to come up with one idea that will help move you from the first to the second. Improvement should be an ongoing goal of every life. *Ultimately, I want you to become your own personality model.* With an understanding of yourself now and what you want to become, you will eventually eliminate any need for either Vince Lombardi or Jillian Michaels as a guide. The objective should be to have all of your decisions based on a personal philosophy toward success, one that is right for you. Begin to move from the person you are to the person you want to be and, in short time, you will no longer need an external model as you implement your plans to reach Level-3 goals.

Thirteen: Think Differently

"You don't have to be Al Capone to transgress—you just have to think. 'In human society,' Mr. Ringold taught us, 'thinking's the greatest transgression of all.'

'Cri-ti-cal think-ing,' Mr. Ringold said, using his knuckles to rap out each of the syllables on his desktop, '—there is the ultimate subversion.'"

Philip Roth, *I Married a Communist*

Perform an Internet search for "most admired companies" and Apple, Google, and Amazon will almost certainly appear near the top of any list. Why? What makes these three businesses so admirable? What is the secret?

One simple answer is that these companies (and a few others that come to mind) have avoided getting stuck in the ruts that are so deadly for traditional businesses. They have remained successful by approaching their operating activities in ever new and unique ways.

- The list of Apple inventions from iPods to iPads is breathtaking. According to *Time* magazine late in 2013, "Look around our smartphone-saturated, cloud-enabled and thoroughly digital world: Apple, many would argue, built the future."

- Google started with a basic Internet search engine that has evolved into a plethora of products from Google maps to Google glass.

- Amazon practically created the current state of Internet commerce.

For me, their success all boils down to a single talent: the management and other employees in these organizations have been able to keep thinking. Not just idle daydreaming but the critical thinking necessary to differentiate themselves from competing companies. They do not rely on products that are mere clones of the current market. Instead, they set out to revolutionize the current market. *For most endeavors, thinking differently from the norm is the secret ingredient that separates the few leaders from the many followers.* Perhaps not surprisingly, near the end of 2013, the total market capitalization (hypothetical market value) for these three companies combined is over $1 trillion.

Ask the people who deal with Apple, Google, or Amazon to explain this amazing track record and one word is almost certain to dominate the conversation: innovation. *What is innovation other than taking the mundane and thinking differently about it?* Innovative thinking is essential if you (yes, YOU) are going to stack the odds for success in your favor. It works for these companies; it can work for you.

Not every organization has an inventive mindset. A few years back I sat at a conference table talking with a business executive (but not from one of the three highlighted companies above). I pitched a new approach for a market that I felt offered significant monetary possibilities. After stating my case, I waited for the questions to rain down. I expected an invigorating give and take. Instead, I received a glum stare followed by a death sentence: "If this idea was as great as you believe, someone else would have already done it by now."

How do you argue against such ridiculous logic? The proposal was not debated on its merits, but rather doomed by the mere fact that it was unique. Such limited thinking often makes entities so risk averse that they become paralyzed. The unwritten motto of too many organizations (and too many people) appears to be: We want innovation as long as nothing has to change.

Creative thinking is essential for success, both in business and in your personal quest to attain Level-3 goals. Change is necessary, but does not have to be outlandish or radical to succeed. Some of the most effective innovations of recent history are easy to overlook. Google has gained a huge following for its periodic "doodles" which first appeared on the opening web page in 1998. The company brags about them on its website:

"Doodles are the fun, surprising, and sometimes spontaneous changes that are made to the Google logo to celebrate holidays, anniversaries, and the lives of famous artists, pioneers, and scientists."

The simplicity of the doodle is hard to exaggerate, but the idea has created enormous value for the company. Millions check them out virtually every day. They are avidly discussed in social media. Anyone could have developed this idea, but Google actually recognized the potential. Imagine the amount of goodwill that would have been lost had a corporate executive declared back in 1998: "If this idea was as great as you believe, someone else would have already done it by now."

If you are struggling to achieve a Level-3 goal, is it time to approach the problem with different thinking?

But, perhaps we should discuss a preliminary question: Can people and organizations be taught to think differently? "Taught" is probably the wrong word here. From my own experiences in the classroom, I have no doubt that critical thinking can be encouraged. We can also nurture, stimulate, and reward it. That is what counts. No one believes that Apple, Google, and Amazon are merely products of random luck, organizations that happened to prosper by accident. They have established an internal environment that openly seeks and promotes innovation. How does that occur? How can you become a more innovative thinker?

When I was growing up, James Thurber was a relatively well-known author and cartoonist (a frequent contributor to *The New Yorker* magazine). I have always greatly admired one of his quotes:

"It is better to know some of the questions than all of the answers."

To start thinking differently, focus on creating better questions for yourself and avoid becoming too restricted by inflexible answers. Like a child asking why the sky is blue, develop a deep curiosity. Resulting insights will eventually help you conquer the walls that block the path to Level-3 goals.

When my children were young and went to a store, I often gave them an assignment: "After we leave, I want you to describe one thing about this business that should be done differently to better serve customers or earn more profits." That is not necessarily an easy task. We tend to view our surroundings as permanent and accept the visible landscape as the only workable arrangement. Not until challenged do we consider the existence of viable alternatives. Luckily, the world is newer for children. They are less inclined to blindly follow a "this is the way it has always been done" mentality. Later, when we exited, I was often amazed by the wisdom of their suggestions for improvement. It was a game to them. Some responses were silly ("free candy at the door"), but many were insightful. The children came up with scores of potential changes because such questions were fun rather than work. *Better questions lead to better thinking.* Socrates made that point quite clearly over 2,400 years ago.

As the children grew older, the game expanded to movies. Whenever we left a theatre, I asked each one to grade the movie. Was it an A+ or a B- or a D or what? If a child judged a movie worthy of praise, he or she had to support that decision. When a lower grade was awarded, the child had to provide one change that should have been made to improve the final product. "You have seen this movie one way. How could it have been done differently and made better?" We welcomed family debates which often continued for the entire trip home.

"How could this have been improved?" is a great question to consider throughout your daily wanderings. It stimulates critical thinking. Let your mind expand to consider the widest possible range of answers. Except for the Ten Commandments, nothing in life is really carved in stone. Almost any service, product, or arrangement can be helped by a bit of innovative questioning. I have no proof, but I suspect that the employees at Apple, Google, and Amazon spend more time seeking out better questions and fewer hours defending the status quo.

I was introduced to one example of different thinking back in college when I read *Cat's Cradle*, a book by Kurt Vonnegut. A large part of the storyline concerns a scientist who invents a new product known as ICE-

NINE. In chapter 20, a colleague of the scientist tries to explain how the idea for ICE-NINE was conceived.

"That old man with spotted hands invited me to think of the several ways in which cannonballs might be stacked on a courthouse lawn, of the several ways in which oranges might be packed into a crate."

What happens, the character speculates, if someone discovers a new and different way to stack cannonballs? Whenever we alter an accepted assumption, does that open up a new world of possibilities? Do we restrict our thinking if we lazily assume that the traditional arrangement of cannonballs (or whatever environment we face) is the only feasible option?

To me, that is the essence of thinking differently—questioning how something as commonplace as cannonballs could be rearranged and what potential advances might arise as a result. Over the years, whenever I encounter a problem in the world around me, I frequently raise my favorite question: Can we stack these cannonballs in some different pattern? I then explain to anyone willing to listen that our range of ideas might be too limited because we have boxed ourselves within the confines of traditional thinking. Maybe the question should always be: How could we change the world and what difference would that make in reaching our ultimate goal?

If you find yourself stuck in a rut, do not worry so much about the shackles of standard answers. Instead, focus on reinventing, or at least reconsidering, the questions you ask yourself. Amelia Earhart grew up in a time when the accepted assumption was: men are capable of flying airplanes, but women are not. Those particular cannonballs were all arranged in one fixed pattern that no one seemed willing to challenge. She changed the question by asking: "Does any reason actually exist that prevents a woman from flying an airplane just as well as a man?" The response is obviously "no" because, in 1932, she became the first female to complete a solo nonstop flight across the Atlantic Ocean just 5 years after Charles Lindbergh first accomplished that feat. She refused to let herself be brainwashed into believing the traditional thinking of that day.

Sally Ride, the first woman in space, and Danica Patrick, the most successful female automobile racer of all time, both had to overcome similar barriers because the standard response was always going to be that "a woman cannot do this." Very recently, Diana Nyad became—at 64—the first person to swim from Cuba to Florida without a shark cage. She succeeded after suffering four previous failures stretching over a 35 year period. But, she persevered and reached her Level-3 goal. These are extraordinarily successful people who did not allow themselves to be trapped by unquestioned assumptions. Figure out a different pattern for those cannonballs and the possibilities become limitless.

Evolution is typically viewed as a physical process. Humans learned to walk on two legs; we developed opposable thumbs. There is also a sociological side to evolution. Society believes that cannonballs can only be stacked in one way. By the same thinking, women are not physically able to perform rigorous activities such as flying a plane or a space ship, racing a high-powered car, or swimming long distances. Those set responses become obsolete when society begins to ask better questions and think differently about the answers.

What issues do you face in life where accepted assumptions have been holding you back? To stack the odds of success in your favor, think differently about the world and question how it should be seen. Consider the mundane and envision its transformation into something wonderful and unique. *Never settle for answers that have not been filtered through insightful questions.*

I want to close this essay by describing a personal experience, one where I did not follow this edict. In my defense, I was young and learned a lesson from my failure. I also had not yet read *Cat's Cradle*. Nevertheless, my lack of critical thinking irritates me even to this day.

When I was in high school, the science teacher announced that each student had to prepare an experiment for the science fair. I wanted to earn an A. Doing well was important. For me, that became a Level-3 goal.

At the time, at least in that region of the world, dentists were beginning to use X-ray technology to locate cavities and other needed dental work. Because of this increased use, people had become wary of the possible health risk. The dental profession cautioned patients to avoid overexposure. Of course, that warning exists to this day.

I visited my family dentist and explained that I wanted to demonstrate that adequate care was important when dental or other X-rays were taken. No one should use the technology excessively. He agreed to assist me in this experiment. I bought three young geraniums. One was physically separated and left unexposed to any X-ray. The second was radiated for a few seconds. The third remained under the X-ray machine for a considerable period of time. To this day, I can remember hearing the dentist say (with some amount of glee), "We are really going to fry this one."

My mistake was that I started with a preconceived answer I was cocky: I just knew the last flower was going to die or at least wilt appreciably and never even questioned that expectation. I had already posted a picture of an outstanding science exhibit in my head. In that mental image, the three flowers were placed side-by-side clearly showing the damage inflicted. They would be flanked by a chart explaining the power and danger of X-rays as proven by the visible difference in the three plants. An A (perhaps an A+) would be my proper reward for an excellent effort.

My assumptions soon proved to be 100 percent incorrect. A week passed and then two and all three geraniums continued to flourish. The "fried" geranium showed no harm at all. It looked wonderful. However, my vision of earning an A was seriously damaged.

Failure is often the result of a thinking process that is too restricted. I had trapped myself by expecting a particular answer and never even considered the validity of the question.

Question: How DANGEROUS is X-ray technology?
Expected answer: If overused, X-rays are extremely dangerous.

After a third week with no physical change, I planted the geraniums in my mother's flower bed and began work on a second experiment that was destined to earn a poor grade.

Years later, I realized the answer was not the problem. When the results were not as anticipated, I should have thought differently about the question. If I had placed the three healthy flowers in a row at the science fair with the following caption, the A would have been mine.

Question: How SAFE is X-ray technology?
Actual answer: Unless very much overused, X-rays are extremely safe.

Locked in to my expectations, I never paused to reconsider the whole idea from beginning to end. Apple, Google, and Amazon have not prospered because of such sloppy thinking. I should have searched for a different way to stack those cannonballs. You should learn from my mistake.

Closing Activity: I have long argued that the world's economy would improve dramatically if a single action were taken. All organizations should be required to create an annual employee award (with a significant cash prize) to be titled "The Weirdest Idea of the Past Year that Worked the Best." Every worker immediately has a good reason to look for innovative ways to create practical benefits. Currently, too many employees lack the motivation to think differently. Incentives do matter. Scores of fantastic ideas undoubtedly remain locked inside heads at every organization and never emerge to make operations more effective. Innovation is needed from everyone, not just a few. A monetary prize should stimulate different thinking on a wide scale. Ideas will pour in from every corner of each company. The best are implemented and become eligible for the next award ceremony.

Of course, organizations cannot be forced to provide prizes for creative thinking. But, you can use this same logic to help develop a mind that is more inclined toward innovation.

The first part of this closing assignment is to study the past year—at work, at home, wherever you have been. Consider all the ideas you produced during those 12 months. Take the time to write them down. Pick the one that best meets both of the above criteria. It has to be weird or unusual. It must have actually worked well. This award is not for theoretical accomplishments. Reflecting on the results of the past helps you evaluate your current level of innovative thinking. Are you in a rut or has your brain been pumping out one great suggestion after another? Thinking (like success) is habit-forming. I used to tell my children: the more ideas you have, the more ideas you will have.

Next, create a computer file titled "Weird Ideas to Increase Productivity." Over the next 12 months, whenever you have a unique thought, type it into this file. Also describe what eventually happens to the idea. Was it implemented and, if so, what was the outcome? Monitor your thinking. Push for results.

During this period, encourage the incubation of new ideas by studying the ordinary aspects of everyday life. Reconsider accepted assumptions. Where can changes be made? Where can you envision improvements? Can you stack the cannonballs in a different pattern; and, if so, what possible avenues does that open? Remember that insightful questions provide the energy to power innovation.

At the end of the year, look back at the "Weird Ideas" file and judge whether the depth of your thinking is improving. Becoming more aware of the innovation process helps stimulate you to think differently as a normal part of life. That is the goal! Creative thinking should not be a special event that happens on occasion, but one that occurs every day on a continuous basis.

Fourteen: The Final Word

Starting a book is relatively simple. An entire world of thoughts, plans, and suggestions lies in front of the author just waiting to be harvested. Concluding a book is much more challenging. After writing tens of thousands of words, how can all of those sentences, paragraphs, and pages be pulled together into an ending that makes sense? How do you avoid sounding trite and repetitive as the flood of words dwindles to a trickle?

Early in the creation of the Harry Potter series, author J. K. Rowling wrote the last chapter of the final book and placed it in a safe deposit box until needed many years later. Any number of reasons might have compelled her to take such action. From that point forward, she had a specific ending. Perhaps she wanted to establish a set finish to guide her writing over those seven long books. With a definite conclusion in place, the storyline had a better chance of maintaining consistency from volume to volume. Or, possibly, Rowling worried that she might not be able to complete the series for some reason. If necessary, this last chapter could be distributed to allow readers to discover what happened to Harry, Hermione, Ron, and the other characters.

When I began work on this book 8 months ago, I never considered starting with the final chapter. In truth, I often did not know where the book was heading. It seemed to have a mind all its own. Michelangelo said that "every block of stone has a statue inside it and it is the task of the sculptor to discover it." That is how I felt during the writing. This book has been my attempt to dig into the topic to figure out what I believe about success. Every day along this path has provided one epiphany after another. If this book was created for my edification, it certainly succeeded. I have learned more than I thought possible about stacking the odds of success in my favor. The words just never looked right on the page until I understood what I believed.

Plus, the process has been a true joy. If the search for success is not fun, you clearly have the wrong Level-3 goals.

In the opening weeks of writing, I did settle on a theme for this final essay. I decided to conclude the book by boiling down the essence of achieving success to a single definitive word. I loved the idea—identifying one word to encompass the multitude of thoughts and suggestions described in these pages. During the months of writing, I maintained a computer file of possible candidates for this recognition. At times, the list contained 25 words or more. In the end, I could never agree with myself on just one. Several were so perfect that any selection appeared arbitrary. Important guidance should never come down to the flip of a coin.

Finally, after considerable internal debate, I chose to highlight four words that seemed to best epitomize the personal quest for success. Focus on these in the following weeks, months, and years and I honestly believe that you (yes, YOU) will begin to experience more success in your life. Not every time but more of the time. And, that is not a trivial accomplishment. The world needs people to seek success and be willing to do the work necessary to achieve it. That can be you. That should be you.

Of course, these words are simply my final four. You can agree with any one of them (or a combination) that best fits your thoughts. Or, better still, come up with your own favorite. What word best exemplifies your search to reach the Level-3 goals of life? If your choice is different from mine, please let me know and include your rationale. I am always interested. Feel free to send an explanation of your word for success to me at Jhoyle (at) cpareviewforfree.com.

Ultimately, I decided to emphasize four words because I want an ending where readers are not stuck with my choices. That only seems fair. When the movie Clue was made 25-30 years ago, several different versions of the final scene were filmed. Apparently, Professor Plum was guilty in some theatres while Miss Scarlet or Colonel Mustard committed the crime in others. On the DVD version, all of the endings are included. Viewers can select the conclusion they prefer. The same option applies to this last chapter. I am presenting four words here that reflect nothing more than my views on achieving success. Inevitably, when stretching out to reach Level-3 goals, the decision as to what you focus on remains in your hands, which is where it should be.

Word One: Journey

In today's world, success is too often associated with wins and losses. Never limit your thinking in that way. Success is not a now-and-then effort designed merely to win games or garner awards. True success cannot be turned off and on like a light switch. That vision is too simplistic. Success is more than gaining recognition as a tennis champion, an award-winning singer, or the like. Too many "successful" people are miserable today because their journey has been strictly one-dimensional. Instead, success should be broadly viewed as a considered philosophy that provides a positive direction for all of life. At its best, success is a guiding principle for our journey—how we live each minute of every day. From the beginning, I have had a goal for this book: to assist in the development of an overall philosophy of success that is right for you.

I remarked in an earlier essay that only two quotations were taped to the wall here in my office. At that time, I wrote about one of those ("If you meet the Buddha, kill the Buddha") but made no mention of the other. Directly in front of me at eye-level slightly above my computer screen is the second message that I see dozens of times each day. I taped those words to that spot many years ago so that they would constantly influence my actions.

"The road to success is always under construction."
Jim Miller

I chose the word "journey" for this final chapter because, as this quote reminds me every day, the process of working toward success is more important than the arrival. Although not grammatically correct, I prefer to classify "success" as an action verb rather than as a static noun. For me, success is not a fixed destination because of the finality in that definition. Success is never final. It is not an object—a prize or recognition—but an ongoing journey that permeates every corner of our existence. Success is the challenge we all face each day in identifying Level-3 goals, determining the best way to attain them, and then doing the necessary work to make it all happen. *Success should become like breathing, something we do every moment as a natural part of life.*

In *The Common Reader*, Virginia Woolf wrote that "the journey is everything." The true satisfaction derived from success is not the result of a final achievement no matter how grand. Rather, it comes from doing our best at each of the million small steps along the path. Too many people place their hopes and aspirations on attaining some end product—one that often fades quickly after being acquired. That type of success has the permanency of melting snow. The real excitement is not in arriving at a conclusion but in the thrill of the chase. If you become too enamored with hitting the finish line in first place, success feels brief and tenuous. When you focus on the process of selecting goals, making plans, visualizing excellent performance, looking for personality models, doing the necessary work, and the like, then life is exciting. You must be a successful person every day if you are going to be a successful person any day. The desire always has to burn; the work always has to be done. John Wooden, the most successful basketball coach of all times, said "make each day your masterpiece."

One of the most stirring descriptions of a person's journey in the quest for success comes from a speech made by Theodore Roosevelt more than 100 years ago.

"It is not the critic who counts; not the man who points out how the strong man stumbles, or where the doer of deeds could have done them better. The credit belongs to the man who is actually in the arena, whose face is marred by dust and sweat and blood; who strives valiantly; who errs, who comes short again and again, because there is no effort without error and shortcoming; but who does actually strive to do the deeds; who knows great enthusiasms, the great devotions; who spends himself in a worthy cause; who at the best knows in the end the triumph of high achievement, and who at the worst, if he fails, at least while daring greatly, so that his place shall never be with those cold and timid souls who neither know victory nor defeat."

Word Two: Believe

A few years back my older son gave me a t-shirt for my birthday along with a 12-inch ruler (which is lying beside me today on this desk). Both had a single word printed on them.

Believe

His explanation was simple: "I thought the message sounded like you." True enough. I like being associated with such an upbeat philosophy. Believing in yourself and the importance of your mission can never ensure success, but lack of belief almost guarantees failure. The thought sounds weirdly redundant but I believe in belief. Over the years, I have administered thousands of exams. I have waited at the classroom door watching the anxious faces of tens of thousands of students readying themselves to match their knowledge against my questions. Such opportunities allow students to prove their efforts are worthy of a good grade. Sadly, too many approach the challenge with absolute resignation rather than rousing faith in their abilities. They sometimes look like prisoners being marched to the guillotine. Bad results seem inevitable. And, not surprisingly, they almost always live down to that expectation. Without belief in yourself, the odds of success are clearly stacked against you.

The one noticeable difference I have observed over the years between success and failure on those thousands of tests is belief. *Believe in yourself and almost no challenge is beyond reach.*

I mentioned the author J. K. Rowling at the beginning of this essay. Her story is well-known. On a train trip in 1990, the idea for a book about Harry Potter, a boy wizard, came to her in a burst of inspiration. During that time, she struggled with a wide range of problems. Her marriage had failed and she was clinically depressed. Her mother had died recently. She held no job and had a dependent child. She subsisted on welfare benefits. Her life seemed destined to be one of poverty and misery. She described herself as "the biggest failure I knew." Nevertheless, Rowling did have an idea for a book and believed in her ability to make the story of a wizard world come alive. In a 2008 commencement address at Harvard, she explained how she rebounded to become one of the best-known and wealthiest people in the world.

"So why do I talk about the benefits of failure? Simply because failure meant a stripping away of the inessential. I stopped pretending to myself that I was anything other than what I was, and began to direct all my energy into finishing the only work that mattered to me. Had I really succeeded at anything else, I might never have found the determination to succeed in the one arena I believed I truly belonged."

Rowling discovered a true Level-3 goal and believed success—despite enormous odds—could be achieved by investing all that she had: time and effort. Her confidence was strong enough to drive the work and provide her with the courage to take the risk. Most people in those dire circumstances would have quickly abandoned such a massive undertaking as foolhardy. Instead, Rowling had the self-discipline to sit for hours in a cafe day after day writing the first Harry Potter book. Success here is no mystery. *The only mystery is her willingness to try and that is the component true belief provides.* Even in those dark days, she retained faith in her capacity to write a great book (and then many more). She shifted the odds of success in her favor. Every story should have such a wonderful ending.

Unfortunately, belief also has a dark side. A fine line runs between confidence ("I have done the needed work and believe I am capable of achieving excellent results") and cockiness ("I am bound to do great regardless of my level of preparation"). Never let yourself get fooled by the difference.

Confidence is the belief that comes naturally when you assess a situation, judge the work required, and then make it happen. Evaluate the facts that matter. Then, be willing to spend the time and exert the effort to conquer every wall you encounter along the way. Carefully judge your talents, and the amount of work you need to do will be obvious. Do that preparation and you have every right to believe in yourself.

Confidence is a wonderful feeling, but cockiness leads to reckless decision-making because risk is not properly evaluated. However, be careful not to overcorrect. Modesty can be just as detrimental if a person becomes overly cautious. In fact, a bit of swagger is helpful. It is empowering. I want my students to have all the confidence in the world when they start a test—not cocky or modest but confident. If they have studied seriously, they have every reason to expect the best. *Success should never be a surprise.* Belief provides the inner fuel to keep the momentum pumping until you achieve each Level-3 goal. That is not cockiness; that is confidence. Dizzy Dean, a legendary baseball player from the 1930s, was well-known for saying "it ain't bragging if you can do it." I like hearing that attitude from my students, but only after they have invested sufficient effort to back up the boast.

Word Three: Urgency

Because they are human beings, college students have a strong tendency to procrastinate. Whether scheduled to write a paper, take a test, or create a presentation, most prefer to find other activities to occupy their hours and days until the last possible minute. As a student told me recently, "If a requirement is not on fire, I've got more interesting things to do with my time." Not surprisingly, when the deadline finally looms large, they are often forced to rush through the process so that results suffer. Every teacher knows that students are likely to upgrade their work if a touch of urgency is added to the daily routine.

- "This information will probably show up on your test."
- "I am thinking about handing out a pop quiz sometime next week."
- "You will be expected to explain the material in the third chapter of the textbook."

In classrooms almost every day, teachers rely on such warnings and 10,000 more like them to motivate students to action. The learning process improves whenever urgency is introduced. Students work harder and are more focused. The message is clear: To be successful, do the work now instead of waiting until it is too late.

The benefit of instilling urgency goes beyond education. On *The Biggest Loser*, Jillian Michaels is successful as a trainer because she gets in the face of her team members and makes dieting and exercise an urgent matter to be taken seriously. They have failed for years in the quest to lose weight. Immediate action is essential. If Michaels exerts only mild pressure, ("Let's all think about eating better when we have enough time.") results will be abysmal. Nothing will be different. No one will lose a pound. To impact the lives of the contestants in a positive manner, she must provide a direct push. She needs to elicit a strong effort right then: "Give me 40 sit-ups and then run a mile. You are never going to lose that weight if you don't stop being lazy. You can do this. Now get to work!" Although intense, her methods are not radical. They are effective. Most winning coaches in every sport use the same type of techniques so their players will feel an urgent need to practice hard every day and perform in games at a high level.

Similar routines are apparent virtually every day in the common experiences of life. A boss introduces the tactic by telling an employee, "I want that report finished and on my desk before you leave tonight." Urgency. A parent relies on the same strategy by warning a child, "There will be no television this evening until you finish your homework." Urgency. William S. Burroughs, a writer best known as a member of the Beat Generation in the 1950s, described this motivation rather succinctly: "Desperation is the raw material of drastic change."

The opposite is equally true. If urgency is eliminated from a project, do not be shocked if forward momentum slows down appreciably. The odds for success only shift in your favor if you keep pushing for immediate progress. That is why the sense of urgency is essential.

When I taught CPA exam review programs, I found that motivation was important to keep the participants on task: "You can avoid sacrifice today, but then you'll miss the benefit tomorrow. You can eat cake today or you can be slimmer tomorrow. In this way, life is simple. That is how it works. You can skip exercising today or you can be stronger tomorrow. You can study today or fail the exam tomorrow. You are an adult. The decision is up to you. Success comes to the person who makes the best use of today. If the goal is important, get started (and do it now)."

After growing up, people often fail to experience the fulfillment in their lives they had expected. They find themselves disappointed and bored without a sense of purpose. That is, at least in part, because they have left behind much of the external motivation system of childhood. No coach or teacher is likely to hang around to push them forward through adult life. They are on their own and life can suddenly seem aimless without outside urgency to provide direction. The void needs to be filled. A life missing urgency can feel a little trivial. Take control. Start looking to identify and then achieve your Level-3 goals. Supply your own urgency.

Why do we require an external force (a teacher, trainer, coach, boss, or parent) to provide the urgency that helps us overcome our tendency to procrastinate? The answer, of course, is that we really do not need outside motivation. As children, we become dependent on having others march us along a chosen path. As adults, that role now belongs to us. In the transition, this change is easy to overlook. *If you have genuine Level-3 goals, a key step in stacking the odds of success in your favor is being able to create your own sense of urgency.* Determine the objective, chart the course, and get to work.

In the 1989 movie *Dead Poets Society*, Robins Williams portrays a high school English teacher at a fancy boarding school. He wants his students to break out of their shells and urges them onward:

"Carpe, carpe diem, seize the day boys, make your lives extraordinary."

Carpe diem, as the quote explains, translates as "seize the day." This Latin term is just another way to point out the need to maintain a level of urgency as we tackle our daily challenges. *No one experiences an extraordinary life through procrastination.*

How can a sense of urgency be created without Jillian Michaels or a coach, a teacher, or your mom? For a lot of adults, the answer to that question is the difference in success and failure.

When I first became a college professor, I wanted to be a great teacher (and still do). Getting by was not good enough. I took notes every day and soon made a startling discovery—the more I prepared for class the better the students learned. In hindsight, that seems rather obvious, but I was young and inexperienced at the time. For me, this logic morphed into "Joe's Theorem for Success," an equation I have explained to countless students over the decades. The theorem states: If X number of hours is required to be average (earn a C for a particular task), then 2X hours are required to be good (earn a B), and 3X to be excellent (earn an A). For any objective you want to accomplish, answer two questions and the necessary level of urgency becomes easier to gauge. First, what grade do you really want? For example, if I am satisfied to be average, I only need to invest X amount of time. But, if a specific goal is so important that I want to perform at an A level, then I must find a way to squeeze out 3X hours of work. Never be naïve; excellence takes time. A shortage of time helps stimulate urgency.

Next, I start every morning by writing down the jobs I want to accomplish that day. I place a single X by each one and estimate the amount of time needed to achieve a grade of C. How long does a specific task take to be mediocre? That is a fascinating question. It might be a half-hour, two hours, or whatever. Finally, I consider each of the listed items one final time and ask myself whether I will be satisfied with average results or if I truly want the outcome to be good (2X amount of time needed) or great (3X).

For me, this daily scheduling brings urgency out of the theoretical and into the practical world. What really must be accomplished today? How much time is needed? Excellent results never happen without a serious commitment. The estimated hours are required, starting immediately. The choice of where to focus energy is mine and not handed down by some outside motivator. For each task, I decide how good I want to be and start putting in the time to reach that goal. The theorem provides a solid approximation of the work needed to achieve success. Knowledge of that time requirement forces me to dig down each day and find the urgency that will get the work started without being hindered by procrastination.

You can do it. You do not need an external motivator to provide urgency. Instead, that essential ingredient must come from inside. Make it happen. Do the work and do it now.

The Final Word: Grit

A number of words qualify for inclusion in this last selection: Determination, perseverance, tenacity, and self-discipline are all wonderful examples. But, I prefer "grit." It conveys the inner toughness people need—both physical and mental—to take on the challenges of a Level-3 goal and do the work to improve the odds for success.

Grit also serves as fair warning that this path will not be an easy one to tread.

Six months ago, a colleague and close friend emailed me a video link and suggested I watch. He assured me that only six minutes were needed, but the time would be well spent. I clicked on the link and up popped a speech delivered by Angela Lee Duckworth at a TED conference in April 2013. Recently, she has become well-known for her research at the University of Pennsylvania on the factors that contribute most to success. Her work is certainly relevant and the findings have sparked considerable interest. Those six minutes have been seen over 2 million times on the Internet. Many viewers probably consider her message to be shocking. I find it liberating.

"One characteristic emerged as a significant predictor of success and it wasn't social intelligence, it wasn't good looks, physical health, and it wasn't IQ. It was grit. Grit is passion and perseverance for very long-term goals. Grit is having stamina. Grit is sticking with your future."

Her research should provide people with a great deal of solace. Success is not reserved strictly for the smart or attractive. It is available to us all. Everyone can be successful, even those not born into wealth and privilege. To improve the odds, set Level-3 goals and then do the work. Stick to it. More than any other characteristic, that intense level of determination offers the best chance for reaching the summit.

As interesting as Duckworth's words are, they are hardly revolutionary. In "What It Takes to be Great," in the October 30, 2006, issue of *Fortune*, Geoffrey Colvin states, "Scientists worldwide have conducted scores of studies since the 1993 publication of a landmark paper by Ericsson and two colleagues, many focusing on sports, music, and chess, in which performance is relatively easy to measure and plot over time. But plenty of additional studies have also examined other fields, including business. The first major conclusion is that nobody is great without work."

Success comes from work and grit is the personality trait that enables a person to fulfill that requirement. Thus, anyone can be successful. That statement really seems too good to be true. But, it reinforces much of what I observed over four decades in the classroom. Students who work hard on a consistent basis are more likely to succeed. That helps explain why some of the smartest students do poorly. Of course, nothing works all the time. Nevertheless, based on my personal experiences, I agree completely with Duckworth: Grit is the number one predictor of success.

As mentioned earlier in this book, I taught a CPA exam review program for 23 years. For 15 Saturdays each fall and another 15 in the spring, 150-200 aspiring CPAs gathered in a room where I pushed them unmercifully for six hours to learn massive amounts of complex materials. During those years, the pass rate was roughly 33 percent on each of the four parts of the exam. The class was long, the work was hard, and the risk of failure was incredibly high. Everyone searched for a secret password that would help ensure success. However, secret passwords really do not exist.

Virtually from the first day, my experiences mirrored Duckworth's research findings. After a few years, I began to mentally classify review course participants into three broad categories.

- **Shooting Stars.** One small group began each semester with hyper excitement. They raved in glowing terms about how much they had looked forward to spending weeks learning all the material and passing the CPA exam. Unfortunately, these candidates almost invariably quit within the first week or two. The whole experience was merely an exciting fantasy for them. They loved to talk about success but, as soon as they faced the hours of monotonous work, the illusion shattered. The fun stopped rather abruptly. I thought of them as shooting stars. They shone brightly for a short time and then flamed out. They had no grit.

- **Yo-Yos.** The efforts of the second group bounced up and down like a yo-yo. One week they were wonderful students—well prepared and engaged. The next Saturday, they seemed lost from the first word. On their bad days, they were distracted and lacked concentration from beginning to end. They occasionally looked a bit hung over. They usually did well until something more interesting came along. Those were the people who skipped class when an important event like a football game was on television. A few passed; most failed. I often referred to the group as having Swiss cheese knowledge. It appeared solid and felt firm, but it contained big holes all the way through. The CPA exam exploited those areas where the knowledge was missing. These participants had some grit but not enough to fill in those holes.

- **Rock Solid.** The third group was present every week from 9 in the morning until 4 in the afternoon—rain or shine. If I held class over for 15 extra minutes, they did not start to squirm. Each week, they turned in homework that showed consistent thought and effort. These candidates appeared to be studying virtually every day. Although not necessarily the smartest people in the room, they were there with a purpose that was firmly in mind. They planned to pass the CPA exam and hoped never to return. And, by far, they were the most successful. I loved working with them. They had plenty of grit.

Are you a shooting star, a yo-yo, or rock solid? Do you really want success or is that just a dream? Do you (yes, YOU) have the necessary grit? If so, I can explain how to stack the odds in your favor. It is no secret. Identify your Level-3 goals, those outcomes that are so important that you are willing to do the challenging work that is required. Look around you for examples of genuine success and figure out what really creates that greatness. Schedule out the tasks to be accomplished. Success never happens by accident; planning is essential. Visualize the individual steps. Mentally, see yourself performing each one and doing it well. Tell yourself stories that will build a positive attitude. Select a personality model to provide guidance for the multitude of decisions that you can never anticipate in advance. Think differently. It is hard to get ahead by thinking like everyone else. Most of all, believe in yourself strongly enough so that you are willing to make the effort every day with an obsessive consistency until you walk away knowing you have done your best.

At the Franklin Institute in Philadelphia, a sign provides Benjamin Franklin's thoughts on what is the equivalent of grit:

"I am a strong believer in luck and I find the harder I work the more I have of it."

Closing Activity: Four years ago, I decided to become a better teacher (a Level-3 goal). I wanted to think more deeply about what I was doing in my classes and how well (or poorly) my tactics were working. I have always had trouble knowing what I believe until I write it down. Somehow the vague notions in my brain are too disjointed and random.

Words structured on a piece of paper are more solid. Lining them up sequentially to form sentences always forces me to separate real ideas from fantasies.

Therefore, to help organize my thinking about teaching and encourage improvement, I started writing a blog. At the time, I expected to compose a few essays and then close down the project. How much could one person possibly have to say about teaching?

I have now written nearly 200 blog entries or approximately 140,000 words. To put that number in perspective, the teaching blog is nearly four times longer than this entire book. I wrote all of those words for my own benefit, but the site has managed to garner over 100,000 page views. Most importantly, at least for me, this writing exercise has helped me become a better teacher. The blog has been a success.

Here is my final assignment. For the next month or so, keep a diary (on paper) or a blog (on the Internet) and write about success. Look at the topic from any perspective you wish, but each entry has to focus on success. One suggestion is to read a page or two in this book and then construct a response. Do you agree with me? What changes do you recommend for my thoughts and suggestions? Think and write: a great combination for improvement.

Write as frequently as possible—every day or 2-3 times per week. This assignment has a single purpose: to provide a formal avenue for you to consider success more deeply. Keep writing for as long as you can. Make it your goal to have at least 30 entries before you even consider stopping. My bet is that this closing exercise will help you (yes, YOU) become a more successful person. Not all of the time but more of the time. That can be you. That should be you.

"May God bless and keep you always
May your wishes all come true
May you always do for others
And let others do for you

May you build a ladder to the stars
And climb on every rung
May you stay
Forever young"
Bob Dylan, *Forever Young*

THANKS!

Many people deserve thanks for helping make this book a reality. No one is more worthy of recognition than Sarah, my wife of 43 years. She has read each of the chapters and provided insightful suggestions and thoughts without seeming to be critical. That is a wonderful talent. More importantly, over all these years, she has been a great partner in conversation. Ideas rarely leap forward fully grown. They require discussion and analysis. The incubation period can be slow and tedious. Sarah has always been there, ready and willing to talk and provide feedback or, in many cases, just listen. Intelligent conversation is hard to beat. And, no matter how strange many of my ideas have been over the years, she has resisted the temptation to make me feel eccentric or foolish.

I also want to thank my business partner Lynn Sheehan who has worked tirelessly to make this project come to life. With help, I wrote the words. Lynn did absolutely everything else. She read the manuscript many times and responded with excellent questions that helped me rethink troubled spots. She provided almost daily encouragement and never seemed to lose faith that I could create an entire book (even when I was not so sure). She set up the entire publishing process. She has directed our marketing efforts. Any real work that had to be done was probably done by Lynn.

In addition, I need to thank my elder son Jamin for creating the front and back covers. Despite a busy schedule at the advertising agency where he works, he was kind enough to produce a brilliant and professional-looking physical vision for the book. He made me look like I knew what I was doing. One piece of advice that I should have given for stacking the odds of success in your favor: Have four extremely talented children and then lean on them to help you with your projects.

I was also lucky enough to have several other people who read parts or all of the manuscript in order to provide me with feedback. Their thoughts were invaluable. They gave me so many helpful suggestions that I could never have discovered on my own. Special thanks to: Susan Bartlett, Steve Chaplin, Krystal Deets, Matt McBride, Jason Palmer, J. P. Payne, Mike Spear, and Kristy Witkowski.

CPA Review for FREE—The Story

Proceeds from the sale of *Don't Just Dream About Success: Stack the Odds in Your Favor* will go to provide financing for CPA Review for FREE. In 2008, Lynn Sheehan, Steve Chaplin, and I formed this operation to help accountants pass the CPA exam without having to incur extravagant costs. Success on this high-stakes exam is necessary to enter the public accounting profession. Unfortunately, review programs often cost several thousand dollars. Many potential candidates never become CPAs because they simply cannot afford to buy such expensive preparatory materials.

To help all future accountants have an adequate opportunity to be successful, we began to provide over 2,400 free questions and answers that are available 24 hours per day 365 days per year. Using this material, many candidates over the years have become CPAs at no cost. We have about 500,000 visits each year to our website. The exam is now global and our traffic comes from around the world. In what is probably the best evidence of our effectiveness, the average visitor stays for over 20 minutes. That is a lot of people working a lot of problems for free. Knowledge is gained; grades are improved. We believe that is a worthy mission. Professions should not have cost barriers.

This book was written as a way to finance the expenses incurred each year to maintain our database and website. Please visit us at www.CPAreviewforFREE.com and also on Facebook.

Thanks very much for your support.